# GET IN!

# FOOTBALL ACCORDING TO
# MARK GOLDBRIDGE

# GET IN!

**EBURY SPOTLIGHT**

1

Ebury Spotlight, an imprint of Ebury Publishing
20 Vauxhall Bridge Road
London SW1V 2SA

Ebury Spotlight is part of the Penguin Random House group of companies whose addresses can be found at global.penguinrandomhouse.com

Penguin
Random House
UK

Mark Goldbridge has asserted his right to be identified as the author of this Work in accordance with the Copyright, Designs and Patents Act 1988

First published by Ebury Spotlight in 2024

www.penguin.co.uk

A CIP catalogue record for this book is available from the British Library

ISBN 9781529920147

Typeset in 11.75/20.5 pt ITC Galliard Std by Jouve (UK), Milton Keynes.

Printed and bound in Great Britain by Clays Ltd, Elcograf S.p.A.

The authorised representative in the EEA is Penguin Random House Ireland, Morrison Chambers, 32 Nassau Street, Dublin D02 YH68

MIX
Paper | Supporting
responsible forestry
FSC
www.fsc.org
FSC® C018179

Penguin Random House is committed to a sustainable future for our business, our readers and our planet. This book is made from Forest Stewardship Council® certified paper.

*To my wife and children. Thank you for giving me the time to grow these wings and fly. It's been an amazing journey. I'm glad I spent it with you xxxx*

# CONTENTS

# PROLOGUE

No matter which team you support, being a football fan is a constant battle against humiliation and disaster. You might expect that because I support 'Glory Glory' Manchester United, I've avoided a lot of hardship. Well, you'd be talking a load of crap. I've almost pissed myself en route to Old Trafford, been threatened on the school bus for telling stories about Roy Keane and been blocked by Gary Lineker on Twitter. There's also my Cold War spy days when I had to secretly trade recordings of Subbuteo games in the playground or face getting my head flushed down the toilet by the school bully. That's all before I set up my own YouTube channel and got called a 'Forest-supporting twat' on a daily basis. And that's just from my fellow United fans . . .

It doesn't really matter who you support. Football is a cruel, cruel game. All of us fans have had moments of shock, disappointment and feeling like a right knobhead. We want

1

our teams to play like a pack of wolves. More often they're a pack of prats. There are so many clowns on the pitch, you'd think the circus was in town. We've endured abject surrenders in the pissing-down rain, watched multimillionaire managers lose the plot ('If I speak . . .') and signed players who couldn't pass a parcel, all to the sound of Michael Owen's 'expert' analysis – all this season after bloody season. It's like watching UK Gold. At times, football has ruined our week, month and even our year. It stings so much, your team might as well be sponsored by Dettol. Why do we do it to ourselves? Surely an afternoon waxing your crack would be time better spent.

It's actually a miracle most of us became fans in the first place. Growing up in the eighties, it wasn't like being a football fan was an easy choice. Hooliganism was rife, the stadiums were crap and most teams' tactics were so prehistoric they could have been managed by Fred Flintstone. Yabba dabba doo! Where's David Attenborough? There's dinosaurs shitting all over the pitch.

Playing the game wasn't much better either. Until leisure centres came along, the best you got was a park covered in dog crap. You'd come home looking like Piers Morgan in *Home Alone 2*. As if that wasn't enough, one time when I was playing football with some mates, a crazy old fella chased us with a knife and tried to pop our ball. Clearly, the locals weren't ready for Goldbridgeball on the mean streets of rural Nottinghamshire.

It all seemed grim. Football was in a bad way. It was as if someone had shit in the pool, and everyone had jumped out. To become a fan, you somehow had to see through all the crap and the Anfield Rap and believe that the game was still beautiful. Somehow, some of us did. We picked up this rusting, rotting turd and saw something that many others didn't. It was still the game of Law, Charlton and Best. It could still be the sport that had given us 'They think it's all over. It is now.' It captivated us, took over our lives, gave us moments of joy, and still kicked us in the balls from time to time. Thanks Sergio Agüero. (Settle down City fans. We'll get to his horrible smug face and boyband wannabee haircut later. The little twat.)

Now I'm older, wiser and wider; there are no cobwebs on me. They don't call me SpiderBridge for nothing. I've learned more than a few lessons along the way. Sharing them in this book has been a lot like therapy – or a colonoscopy. Either way, I hope you can learn from my (many) mistakes and save yourself from looking like a right knobhead. You might even learn to enjoy watching your team from time to time.

So, bring your chips, 'cos I'm going to get salty, as we'll get into turning my football addiction into a career, doing a runner at the prospect of supporting Coventry City and the time McFred double-teamed me. No, not like that. Honestly. Minds like sewers, you lot. We'll also take a trip down memory lane, wallowing in the glory of Saint and Greavsie, The

Lightning Seeds and the soothing sound of *Grandstand*'s vidiprinter – forget your spa music when you're in the bath; just whack that on.

There's a lot to get through, so take my hand like an over-eager mascot and walk with me out of the tunnel into the glaring floodlights of what it means to be a fan . . .

. . . and how to survive it.

# 1

# INDIANA JONES AND THE FOOTBALL TEAM OF DOOM

When I was nine, my mum took me to the cinema to see *Indiana Jones and the Last Crusade*. Like Postman Pat, she well and truly delivered. For two whole hours, I sat mesmerised as Harrison Ford teamed up with Sean Connery to do battle with the Nazis and search for the Holy Grail. Finally, Indy and the Nazis track the treasure down to a mountain cave. There, an old knight from the Crusades gives them a choice.

In a room full of different cups of every description, he tells them to pick the one they think is the Grail and to take a sip of water from it. If they choose wisely, they'll receive eternal life. If they choose poorly, they'll die an instant death. The villain picks a gold goblet covered in jewels. It seems a good choice. Bloody wrong! I watched in horror as he took a sip and quickly transformed into a Wish version of Gary Lineker, before melting into a skeleton and collapsing into a pile of dust. Jesus. I nearly shat myself. Thankfully, Indy is far shrewder than his adversary. Picking up a small, battered, rusting cup, he takes a sip and is granted eternal life, a bit like Steve Bruce's managerial career.

Anyway, I'm sure you're thinking, *Lovely story, Mark, but what the bloody hell does this have to do with anything?* Calm down. Hold your horses. It's called an analogy, and the point is this choice is kind of like the one we get given to us as kids when it's time to decide what football team we're going to support. Choose wisely, and it's the equivalent of listening to classic Oasis and having a cooked breakfast every day for the rest of your life. A feast for the eyes and the ears. But choose poorly, and you're destined to be crying in the bogs at work after another disasterclass from a bunch of overpaid shithouses.

You don't understand what you're getting into at such a tender age. It's a dangerous time. This sort of decision should come with a warning. Or at least a theory test, like you have to pass before taking your driving test.

Question 1: Do you hate yourself? If yes, please see question 2.

Question 2: Congratulations. You now support Mansfield Town.

Science even backs this up. Studies have proven that fans who are happy with their club have higher levels of self-esteem, more positive feelings and lower levels of loneliness and alienation. No shit, Sherlock! Getting this decision right is absolutely crucial. You can't go into it like a blindfolded cat in a room full of rocking chairs. You've got to have your wits about you if you want to keep your tail.

Few of us take such care, though. Often, the choice of team we'll support for the rest of our lives is left to fate. It's like Timo Werner bearing down on goal, shutting his eyes, swinging at the ball and hoping for the best. And just like that. Bang! Rather than hitting the back of the net, our choices end up hitting some poor grandad in row Z. I certainly had a lot of choices, all of which would have made some sort of sense. But nothing is straightforward as a football fan. If you don't want to ruin your life, then park your bums and read on.

## THE GLORY SUPPORTER

Most kids want to support a winner. They want to revel in watching the best players in the world winning the biggest trophies. Like Billy Big Bollocks, they wear their replica shirt with pride, sticking out their chest like they've got a Wonderbra on. 'Ooooh, look at me supporting the best team.'

I get it. It's like going on *Blind Date* but being shown your options before you arrive. No *Surprise Surprise*, thank you very much, Cilla. I'm taking number 3, Carol, the former Miss Cardiff, on an all-expenses-paid weekend to Magaluf. What bloody idiot isn't going to pick the best of the crop? But calm down. Looks aren't everything, you know. And when it comes to football, it's not as easy as it seems. Today's winner is tomorrow's loser. You need to exercise some caution. For example, I could easily have been a Coventry City fan.

One boiling hot day in May 1987, I was playing with my *Star Wars* figures in the back garden.

'I am your father, Luke.'

'Piss off, you heavy-breathing prat.'

You get the picture.

Anyway, after getting overexcited, I went inside for a drink and heard the television blaring from the living room. Poking my head around the corner, I saw my dad sitting on the sofa, intently watching the small, flickering screen. Suddenly a huge cheer erupted as a team in white and a team in sky blue stepped out onto the pristine green pitch. It was the 1987 FA Cup final. Coventry vs Spurs.

My awareness of football on the TV at that time was virtually zero. It might as well have been the Hungarian tiddlywinks championship. So, when I saw that my dad was watching a match, there was no competition for an afternoon of Han Solo getting jiggy with Princess Leia in the garden. But for some reason, I kept thinking about what I had seen on the telly. I was drawn to it, like a Premier League footballer to the Saudi League.

Every ten minutes or so, I kept popping back in to see what was going on. As the game unfolded, my dad was getting increasingly excited, jumping around like Mikel Arteta begging for a throw-in. I'd never seen my dad like this before. This strange game was making him do weird things, like it was magic. I took a seat, wondering if the magic would rub off on me. It did.

As my dad shouted and cheered, so did I. I didn't know why I was doing it, but it felt good. It was infectious. Looking back now, maybe a part of me was trying to please my dad. It was a chance to be close to him and do something together. Suddenly, we were a team, like Ant and Dec.

I also started to pay attention to the players. One in particular stood out to me. The winger for the white team had very short shorts and a long flowing mullet. *What the bloody hell have we got here*, I thought. He was quick and skilful, going past players like they were statues, or Sheffield United players. It was Chris Waddle, who set up Clive Allen for his 49th goal of the season.

My dad didn't cheer for that goal, though. Nor did he cheer when Gary Mabbutt scored. However, for all three Coventry goals, he stood up and roared as Spurs showed all the resistance of a poppadom trying to stop a bowling ball. It scared me at first, but by the final Coventry goal, I was on my feet as well. When the final whistle blew, I watched as the white players sank to their knees in despair. They'd lost the game 3–2. My dad smiled. So did I. I liked having this moment together. I had no idea that my dad was a Chelsea fan, and he was particularly pleased that a good Spurs team had just bottled the Cup final. Trigger warning, Spurs fans. We'll be talking about 'Spursiness' in a bit . . .

This was the day when I not only became fully aware of watching live football matches, but found that I liked it. This was the promised land. I was hooked, eagerly looking for my next fix, like Harry Redknapp on transfer deadline day. And my first taste of it was watching Coventry City lift a big trophy in front of a packed Wembley. To my immature eyes, Coventry might as well have been Brazil. I'd even heard of the city. It wasn't that far away from where I lived, a 40-minute drive at most. Could Coventry City be the promised land for an impressionable young Goldbridge? Looking back, I was like a young squirrel trying to cross the M25.

How was a young kid to know that the 1987 Cup final would be the greatest day in Coventry City's history though? That since 2000 the club would spend 23 years and counting bobbing around the lower leagues, sometimes even having to groundshare with Northampton Town. Thank Christ for divine intervention. Even as a kid, I must have had some radar that told me, 'Stay away from them, son. They're no good for you.' Sort of like the Charley Says adverts we were bombarded with as kids in the eighties that warned us not to speak to strangers. Instead of a stranger coming up to you and asking if you'd like to see some puppies, they'd ask, 'Do you fancy coming with me to watch Coventry?' Clearly, that's a red flag.

Despite their team losing the final, I might have become a Spurs fan. I had already taken a liking to Chris Waddle, who was not only a football superstar but appeared on *Top of the Pops* duetting with Glenn Hoddle for their single 'Diamond Lights'. As far as football songs go, this one is right up there with Gazza's 'Fog on the Tyne' (that's a compliment, by the way).

Spurs also had Clive Allen, the best striker in the country at the time. He was as sharp as barbers' scissors that season. Everyone tugs off Haaland and his goal record, but you're having a laugh doing that for Spurs. Yet while I appreciated this, I felt no natural connection to Spurs. Thankfully I'd been educated in their full Bottlejob FC glory in one of the first games I'd ever seen, where they embarrassed themselves by losing to an underdog side in a major final. This was all the warning I needed. Thank God. Imagine being a Spurs fan for the rest of your life. Constant disappointment. 'Don't worry, lads, it's only Spurs.' What does that level of bottling do to a person over a lifetime? You must end up with massive trust issues. Like a porn star going to work in the morning. You just know you're going to get screwed one way or another . . .

If you think I'm picking on you, Spurs fans, let's look at the facts. Since the Premier League began in 1992 Spurs have lost more points from winning positions than any other team. I can't be blamed for this. Take it up with Christian Gross.

Anyway, while Coventry and Spurs were both showing a bit of leg for any potential glory supporter, there was another club that was the real deal, looming large, like the Death Star. When I started at Colston Bassett Primary School in 1987, I quickly found that most boys in my class were football fans. Lovely jubbly. But if I wanted to be top dog, there was a very simple choice I would have to make: support Liverpool.

At the time, Liverpool was dominant. Since the mid-1960s, the club had won the league 11 times, the European Cup four times and the UEFA Cup twice. Between 1981 and 1984, Liverpool won the League Cup four years on the trot. Yes, they were sickeningly good. And if I wanted to sit with the cool kids, all I had to do was pledge allegiance to Kenny Dalglish and the 'Anfield Rap'. I'm trying not to give myself a heart attack thinking of this.

Thankfully, like a turkey when he sees the Christmas Coca-Cola lorries, I hated them. Hated them! Their horrible Candy kits; Dalglish, Rush and bloody Barnes; Steve McMahon making a prat of himself on the 'Anfield Rap' – and the arrogance of thinking they were going to win all the time. Absolutely disgusting. Yeah. Not for me. No thanks. Not even if it meant I had to spend my break times with the computer gang. Being popular wasn't worth that much to me.

I didn't even see Liverpool as a rival back then. I just couldn't connect to the team in any way. It would have felt like I was selling out, not being true to myself just to win over a few mates. You can lead a horse to water, but sometimes, it won't want to drink. I was that horse. I'd rather be taken to the glue factory than to Anfield. Talk about dodging a bullet. I'd rather walk alone.

## THE LOCAL TEAM

If you didn't fancy supporting one of the glory teams and wanted to avoid being inside with the computer club nerds, there was, thankfully, another socially acceptable choice: support the local team.

For me, this was either Nottingham Forest or Notts County, as the City Ground and Meadow Lane are both about a 20-minute car drive from the village where I lived. Forest not only played in the top division but, in 1979 and 1980, won back-to-back European Cups under Brian Clough. I know. It's hard to believe now, just like it's hard to believe Eric Dier was a regular for England. There'd been a few dry years since, but Forest was still regarded as one of the best teams in the country, boasting a side full of top players, such as Stuart Pearce, Des Walker, Nigel Clough and Neil Webb. Ooh, la la! For all these reasons, supporting Forest was as alluring as a night in with the wife and a Chinese takeaway. (That's a good thing, by the way.)

In fact, the first football match I ever attended was Nottingham Forest vs Newcastle on New Year's Day 1988. I went with my dad, and I vividly remember that Newcastle had a Brazilian playing for them called Mirandinha. He was the first Brazilian to play in the top flight, having signed from Palmeiras for £575,000 just a few months before. He'd also scored for Brazil against England at Wembley, so all eyes were on him. To have a foreign player, let alone a Brazilian, in the First Division back then was like seeing an open-top bus trophy parade in Tottenham – a real rarity. So for Mirandinha to play for Cheryl Cole FC was mental. I mean, his agent completely fucked him there, let's be honest. It'd be like Vinicius Junior signing for Luton. It's no wonder he didn't last long.

He didn't disappoint that day, though, as he scored in a 2–0 win for the Magpies. Gazza also played and scored, but I can't remember anything about him now or little about the game. I suppose that tells you everything you need to know. My dad took me to a few Forest games when I was a kid, but while I enjoyed going I never felt any real connection – much like Antonio Conte at Spurs. I was there. I probably liked it for a bit. But it never really felt like a good fit. That's how I felt about Forest. It was all pleasant enough and, like a KitKat stolen from the cupboard before dinner, my interest in the club filled a hole for a time, but it never grabbed me, no matter what those prats on social media will tell you. In fact, let's clear this up once and for all. I've NEVER supported

Forest. Never! Alright! For some reason, the haters get harder than a groom on his wedding night at the thought of me supporting Forest. If I had an OnlyFans account of me wearing Forest shirts I'm telling you I'd be a bloody millionaire. Now shut up and sit down.

While my dad took me to Forest games because the club was local and doing well at the time, he could have also taken me to Notts County. Meadow Lane is directly across the River Trent from the City Ground, so there would have been no further distance to travel. In the late eighties and early nineties, County was also a team on the rise, slam-dunking the opposition like digestives into a cup of milky tea. In three successive seasons under Neil Warnock, he took the club from the third division into the top flight. It was power-shower football, and then some.

Quite a few of the kids in my class went to County games. They were part-time wankers, though. County was just their bit on the side. Something for a bit of cheap fun on the weekend. No one needed to know. They might as well have been called Ryan Giggs FC. 'Keep it to yourself, yeah. I'll give you a call.' Bunch of dirty stop-outs. During the week, they'd support a big club like Liverpool, then come crawling back for their fix.

For some reason, my dad never took me to a County game, so there was never any danger of supporting them. Good parenting there, Dad. My eyes are bleached enough.

Since those halcyon days, County has hurtled down the divisions and even spent a spell in the National League. The club is back in League Two now, though, and doing pretty well. However, I can't say that missing out on supporting County has ever given me sleepless nights.

## THE FAMILY TEAM

If you didn't want to be a glory supporter, or support your local team, then as far as popularity in school went, you were like pineapple on pizza. A total outcast. Although, there was still another option. You could just about save some face if you supported the same team as your dad. Yet even this could be the equivalent of wearing clown pants to school. One kid in my class supported Ipswich. He might as well have painted himself orange and told us he was an Oompa Loompa. Still, while I couldn't sit next to him and risk becoming a social leper, I admired him for not succumbing to the charms of Liverpool.

Like I said, my dad was a Chelsea fan. Unlike some fathers, he never forced this on me. I think he tried in other ways, though. He always left loads of old Chelsea programmes lying around the house or just casually left them on my bed.

'Oh sorry, Mark, I didn't realise I'd left my Cup Winners' Cup final programme on your pillow.'

For fuck's sake, Dad. At least make it *Readers' Wives*.

To be fair, I used to love reading them and learning about players like Peter Osgood, Alan Hudson and Ron 'Chopper' Harris. However, by the late 1980s, the glory years for Chelsea had well and truly faded.

For a while, things on the pitch weren't so bad. The club got promoted back to the First Division in 1984 and had a sprinkling of big-name players like Kerry Dixon, David Speedie and Pat Nevin. In the 1985/1986 season Chelsea even pushed Liverpool for the title, when in March they were just four points off the top, with two games in hand, before collapsing, going on to win just one point from the final five games. Bunch of bloody bottlers. Yet, by the time I became interested in football, Chelsea was far from its glory days. The club would soon be relegated, again, and that wasn't even the worst of its problems.

Things got so bad at Chelsea in the late eighties that the club had to resort to raising money by letting locals park their cars behind the goal! Look it up, I'm not even joking. When Chelsea played at Stamford Bridge there were regularly ten to twenty cars parked behind the goal. Heading in to London to do some Christmas shopping? Park at our west London location for a fiver. And don't worry about the ball hitting your car, our strikers couldn't hit the ocean from a boat!

In short, Chelsea's prospects in the eighties were lower than a worm's arse. It's no surprise that my dad never asked,

'Hey, Mark, do you fancy a Saturday afternoon in London watching posh people park their cars?'

No thanks, Dad. I'd rather watch the grass grow at home.

## THE TWIST OF FATE

Sometimes, there's no rhyme or reason to the team we support. It just ends up happening. Like Scott McTominay, you end up stumbling around Old Trafford, wondering how the hell you ended up there.

When I was seven, my primary school decided to put together a school football team. C'est magnifique! But there was a problem. We didn't have a kit. Then, some clever clogs had a bright idea. Our parents were asked to supply us with a blue kit because the school colours were blue. Genius. And thank Christ. This counted Forest and Liverpool out. However, I'd seen one of the kids in the playground wearing a royal blue shirt with a white V-neck and the word 'Sharp' in white writing across the front. God, it was sexy. I didn't realise it was the Manchester United third kit. I just needed a blue football shirt, preferably one I thought looked cool. This ticked all the boxes.

Gran offered to sew me one, but with the memory of her attempt at a shepherd's cloak in the previous year's Nativity play still fresh in my mind, I kindly declined. The trauma of those tight brown hot pants still lives with me to this day. Thankfully, after providing a detailed description, Mum promised to buy the shirt from a sports shop in Nottingham the next day. How hard could it be? This isn't *The Apprentice*, is it? In fairness, she did buy a blue shirt with a white V-neck collar and the white writing of an electronics company across the front. The only problem was, it didn't look like the one my friend had been wearing. Instead of 'Sharp', the writing said 'NEC'. She'd only bought me a bloody Everton kit! Bloody hell, Mum! If you made that mistake today, a kid would probably call the NSPCC. And so would I if I hadn't just spent my pocket money on a packet of strawberry Chewits. Despite this clusterfuck, I was still thrilled. The team didn't matter to me at the time. It was blue, and my first football top, so I loved it.

It was not only a great kit, but Everton, under Howard Kendall, was one of the best teams in the country. The club had won the league in '85 and '87, and came runners-up in 1986. It had also won the FA Cup in 1984 and the European Cup Winners' Cup in 1985. It's a wonder Everton didn't win more with a squad that included the likes of Neville Southall, Kevin Ratcliffe, Peter Reid, Trevor Steven, Gary Lineker, Adrian Heath and Graeme Sharp. In 1988, the club even broke the British transfer record, spending £2.2 million to sign Tony Cottee from West Ham. I'm afraid you had your pants pulled down there, lads. For the younger generation he was as good a striker as he is a pundit. And we'll leave it there.

Anyway, for some reason, while I happily wore the kit, I never came close to becoming a Toffee. Maybe it's because no one else in my school supported them, or perhaps because I didn't know enough about the club to have any sort of connection. Either way, I definitely saved myself from a lifetime of pain there. The thought of supporting Everton goes through me like a box of All-Bran.

Since those glory days in the 1980s, Everton have only won one major trophy, the FA Cup in 1995 (thanks for that, Paul Rideout). As I'm writing, the club's prospects haven't exactly improved either. I mean, any team with Ashley Young as a starting full-back in 2024 isn't a serious club – it's like asking Ronald McDonald to babysit your cow. Although, to be fair, having six points deducted doesn't help. And before you Toffees start sliding into my DMs, giving it the big one, Goodison Park is one of my favourite stadiums. I love visiting it. Not only because United usually picks up three points and score worldies (thanks, Garnacho) but because it's one of the last of its kind. I'll be gutted when you move to your fancy new stadium, especially since it'll make Old Trafford look like a derelict drug den.

Nevertheless, once more, I had somehow dodged a bullet. Everton was in the bin, where it belonged. Yet I was still without a team to support, and I was running out of options.

## THE CHOSEN ONE

In 1986, my parents separated. This saw me, my younger sister and my mum move in with my grandparents for a bit. However, this suddenly had a big upside.

My grandad was obsessed with Manchester United. Growing up, his idol was Duncan Edwards, the 18-year-old superstar who, but for Munich, might easily have become the best footballer of all time. That's certainly how my grandad saw it. Duncan was big and strong, yet was quick, and could play in any position, including in goal! He'd talk about Duncan Edwards for hours, as well as the Busby Babes and the holy trinity: Law, Best and Charlton.

While he'd talk about his heroes, I also got a chance to see them in action. The late eighties and early nineties were the golden age for football videos. Before YouTube, this is how football fans got their fix in between games. My grandad quickly bought all of the United ones, things like *United's Top 100 Goals* or *The George Best Story*. In the winter, I'd get home from school and, more often than not, I'd find him sitting in the living room, with the fire on, watching a United video. We only had one telly in the house back then, and going outside to play wasn't an option because it was pissing it down, so I began to join him. Forget *Neighbours*. No script for Scott and Charlene could match this.

I quickly learned how Old Trafford was bombed during the Second World War, forcing the club to groundshare with Man City to survive. With things getting desperate, the untested Matt Busby, a former Liverpool player, was appointed as manager, along with Jimmy Murphy as his assistant. They didn't have a pot to piss in, so they had no option but to focus on the youth system in the hope of putting together a winning team.

Scouring the country for talent, Murphy helped bring the likes of Duncan Edwards, Bobby Charlton, Eddie Colman, Tommy Taylor, David Pegg, Roger Byrne, Dennis Viollet and many others into the team. It's a joke, really. With an average age of 21, the new look United team won the league in 1956 and 1957 and the players were soon christened the 'Busby Babes'. My grandad would tell me this was the most exciting football team he had ever seen. They looked destined to dominate English and European football for the next decade and more. But then, disaster struck.

On 6 February 1958, as the team stopped over in Munich while flying home from beating Red Star Belgrade in Serbia (then Yugoslavia), a result that saw them reach the semi-finals of the European Cup, the aircraft crashed on the runway. This disastrous incident led to the deaths of 23 of the 44 on board. In a stroke, most of the 'Babes' were wiped out, including superstar Duncan Edwards. Meanwhile, Matt Busby clung to life, with many not expecting him to survive.

After such a tragedy, it seemed impossible to think that the club would rise again. But somehow, Busby regained his health and, along with survivor Bobby Charlton, focused on his dream: winning the European Cup. Over the next decade, a new and exciting team emerged, featuring the likes of George Best and Denis Law. Together, they would take United to the promised land, finally winning the European Cup in 1968. Munich survivor Bobby Charlton scored in the 4–1 win over Benfica, completing one of the most remarkable stories in sport. I was captivated by it all. It was like a movie. The tragedy. The triumph. The whole romanticism that surrounded the club, along with a long list of iconic players who played with flair and swagger.

However, since then, the club had gone backwards. Six years after winning the European Cup in 1968, United were relegated, with Man City putting the nail in the bloody coffin. Adding insult to injury, the winning goal was scored by former United star Denis Law, with a back-heel. FFS, Denis! He gets a pass, though, as he refused to celebrate and looked genuinely distraught, so much so that he was substituted soon after.

United was at least back in the top flight a year later, and was soon winning trophies again, scooping up the FA Cup in 1977, 1983 and 1985. Big Ron Atkinson had also arrived as manager, bringing a bit of va-va-voom back, along with the signing of skipper Bryan Robson. Despite this, Big Ron was unable to win the league title, which the club had last won in 1967. While he achieved five successive top-four finishes, by November 1986 United was left floundering in the bottom three. Thanks and all, Ron, but it was time for the club to post a photo of a corner flag.

His replacement was Alex Ferguson. Yeah, I know, pass the gravy boat. But hold on a minute. Despite the dominance of Celtic and Rangers, he'd done bloody well in Scotland with Aberdeen, winning three league titles, four Scottish Cups and the European Cup Winners' Cup in 1983, when they improbably beat Real Madrid in the final. It was a phenomenal record. A bit like Mr Blobby keeping Take That and East 17 off the top of the Christmas charts in 1993. Still, Fergie was untested in England and endured a difficult first season at United, finishing in 11th place. As things stood, United still looked far from winning the league, Old Trafford was crumbling and there were far more glamorous teams out there to support – not least Liverpool, Everton, Forest and even Spurs.

Following United back then was no guarantee of glory. It wasn't the fashionable or popular choice, but I just felt in my bones that this was my club. Like a Pot Noodle on a cold day, it felt like a good combo. I'd never had that feeling before. Of course, my grandad supporting United and being surrounded by United memorabilia and videos was a big nudge in the right direction. But it was the incredible story surrounding the club that truly captivated me. It was like all the fairy tales you loved as a kid. Your lead character faces heartache, doom and destruction, then somehow triumphs over adversity, by doing things the right way and with class and dignity. That's how I saw it, anyway.

At the end of the day, I'd done my homework. As any fan should, I'd weighed up my options. I'd ignored the prospect of approval by my peers. I hadn't been seduced by glory or family pressure. I'd patiently waited for my club to come to me. Like Indy, I'd chosen the rusting, battered cup. It turned out to be my Holy Grail.

# 2

# TRANSFERS

There's a turd in the pool. Get out! Get out! But sometimes you can't. Sometimes you've just got to keep swimming in that shitty water and pretend that it's alright. It's like when your club signs a new player. All those hopes and expectations, only to find they're as useful as a plumber on the *Titanic*. You don't know whether to laugh or cry. It's Harry Potter and the Chamber of Transfer Fuck-Ups. Your scouts are spending more time at the hide-and-seek championships than watching football matches. And this isn't *FIFA*. You can't just bin them off. They're human beings who are just really shit at football.

Transfer deadline day is the worst. For most of us, it's like the shittest version of Christmas Day. After months of hype and hope, you rush down the stairs in your He-Man pyjamas to see a package under the tree that looks suspiciously like Robert Lewandowski. You've waited months for this. You've even conned Santa into putting you on the good list. Swivel on that Santa, ya fat prick. But when you hurriedly rip off the wrapping paper, a smiling Odion Ighalo jumps out at you instead.

'I love Manchester United.'

'Get back in the box, you knobhead. You're going back to the North Pole.'

Your mum steps in.

'Mark, why are you crying? I thought you wanted a new centre forward?'

'You don't know me at all, do you!?'

And off you go, stomping back up the stairs, feeling stupid, a bellyful of pain and regret. Dear. Dear. Dear. Beam me up, Scottie. I'm fucking done.

But there are ways to avoid feeling like a prat. To stop being taken in by fake news, shit signings and players who stomp all over your fragile heart. To take you from the depths of despair to a happy salmon leaping into a beautiful clear ocean.

Let's rip the plaster off together . . . 1, 2, 3!

## KNOW YOUR SOURCES

When I was 11, I lived in a small village called Cropwell Bishop, which was about a ten-minute walk away from another village called Cropwell Butler. The paper round between the two villages was highly sought after. All the kids wanted it. For that, you got 25 smackeroos a week! Let me tell you, for a kid in the early nineties, that was some serious money. Don't worry about the school dinner money this week, Mum. I've got it covered. And there'd still be enough left over for an Ace of Base single in Woolworths and a few packs of Premier League stickers.

While I set my eyes on the Cropwell Butler paper round, I knew that first I had to earn my stripes. I therefore started off at the bottom, doing some crappy round in the council estates, getting up at 6am, in all weathers, barely making £8 a week. Unlike other kids doing the rounds, though, I was smart. I knew it wasn't enough just to be good at your job. You had to work the system. You had to be ruthless. You had to be like Ray Liotta in *Goodfellas*. Hardworking, everyone's friend and always looking out for numero uno.

'As far back as I can remember, I've always wanted that paper round. To me, getting that paper round was like being the President of the United States.'

But there are no friends in the paper round world. Let this story be a lesson to you.

Most of my rivals thought the guy who owned the news-agent's would award the Cropwell Butler round on merit. That was true, but I worked out that you also had to befriend the kid who was currently doing the round. When he stepped down he might put in a good word with the big man. It didn't matter that poor old Tom Davies had been up since 5am delivering papers in the pissing-down rain. Cry me a river, Tom. As long as the man on the inside vouched for you, you were in. It really was like *Goodfellas*. There was a system in place. And I really wanted to be a made man.

So, I did my homework. Nothing escaped my attention. I was like Gail Platt in *Corrie*, peering through lace curtains, poking my nose in where it wasn't wanted. No detail was too small. I'd root through the bins if I had to. Finally, I noticed that the boy who currently did the round had a dog. By happy coincidence, so did I. This was my way in. After some small talk, I arranged for us to walk our dogs together, trying to act all calm and normal. Things weren't so easy, though. He was a Liverpool fan, so when he would tell me Stig Inge Bjørnebye was better than Denis Irwin, I just had to bite my tongue. *Don't blow it now, Mark . . . Deep breaths.* I was like Johnny Depp in *Donnie Brasco*. I couldn't blow my cover.

Thankfully, it was all worth it. When he stepped down, he put in a good word, and the round, and £25 a week, was mine. Come to Poppa. Justice Jam on toast. Poor Tom Davies. What can I tell you, kid? The world ain't fair! 'Fuhgedda-boudit!'

Honestly, I know now how footballers feel when Saudi Arabia comes calling. The jump in money was incredible, as was the jump in status. Suddenly, I was the top dog. The Cristiano Ronaldo of the newspaper round. Everyone wants to be your friend, and, like a Roman emperor, you have the power to make dreams come true. But there was also something I hadn't considered; this newspaper round made me the Fabrizio Romano of my school.

As the round involved more travelling than the others, I always had to be the first at the shop to pick up the papers. Back then, this is where almost all football transfer news came from. There was no internet for your fix. The newspaper journos were gods. So, when I picked up the bag of papers at 5am, I would quickly scan the back pages and know what was happening in the football world before most of my friends had had their Coco Pops. Not only was this a thrill but it also meant I became the transfer guru. I virtually ended up doing press conferences on the school bus. And there was one transfer that made my reputation.

In the summer of 1993, Roy Keane was one of the hottest properties in British football. Luckily for me, I saw him play first-hand when my dad took me to watch Forest Signed for £47,000 from Cobh Ramblers in Ireland, it was quickly clear that Keane was a bloody monster. He could run all day, was tough, but could also keep the ball as well as anyone. In his early days, he also had an eye for goal. He was a hero in Nottingham and it was no surprise when high-flying Blackburn Rovers came calling.

Bankrolled by their benefactor Jack Walker, Blackburn was the Man City of their day. It's hard to imagine now, but back then, the club was lighting cigars with £50 notes. It had the financial power to blow most other clubs out of the water and was already stockpiling the league's best talent. When Alan Shearer became available the previous summer, United had been keen, but once Blackburn bid a record fee, it was curtains. We just couldn't compete with that sort of money. It was so bloody annoying. One minute, you'd never even bloody heard of Blackburn; the next, they were outspending everybody. Get back to oblivion where you belong, you dickheads. You're ruining it for everyone.

With this in mind, when news broke that Blackburn had made a record bid for Keane, everyone thought it was game over. It was reported that Keane had also met with Blackburn manager Kenny Dalglish and shaken hands. It was a done deal. Turn the bloody lights off. Bastard, bloody Blackburn! So, when I rose at 6am on 19 July 1993 and collected the newspapers, I was stunned to read that Keane had signed for Manchester United for a British record transfer fee.

Shamone motherfucker! I couldn't believe it. Almost out of the blue, one of the country's best players was signing for my team. This wasn't a rumour. The deal was done. Dalglish might have shaken hands with Keane, but a contract hadn't been signed. Schoolboy error, Kenny! While he went off on his holidays, Fergie swooped. He didn't let Keane out of his sight until he signed on the dotted line. Wake me up before you bloody go go!

As the summer sun rose on the horizon, I remember a warm feeling growing inside, not just at the transfer but at being one of the first to know. I probably felt like Sir Alex when he saw Paul Scholes for the first time. You just know it's all going to be alright.

I completed the round in record time that morning, desperate to be the first on the school bus to break the news. There were always other knobheads trying to muscle in on my turf, and this was my Martine McCutcheon moment. I'd been up since 5am, for fuck's sake. I couldn't let some other kid take all the glory. Sadly, I was far from the hero I had envisaged. It was an early experience of what I would one day face on Twitter if I dared mention a surprise transfer story. Shock. Anger. Name-calling.

'Stop talking shit, you dickhead. Keane's already signed for Blackburn.'

'He hasn't. He's signed for United.'

'Why are you lying? Hey, everyone, Mark's lying 'cos he's got a small knob.'

The state of transfer discourse has continued to go downhill ever since. Nevertheless, despite the fear of having half my underwear rammed up my arse, I didn't back down. I knew I was right. This wasn't some 'exclusive' story in the *Sun*. This was the bloody *Times*! They wouldn't lie, would they?

Quickly, word got around. Other sources were checked. There were muffled whispers in the playground and sly glances in my direction. The top boys stopped polishing their knuckle-dusters. Finally, everyone realised that I had indeed been speaking the truth. There were no official apologies, but suddenly, I was like Don Corleone on his daughter's wedding day. People would seek me out for a private one-on-one.

'Hey, Mark, what was the transfer fee again?'

'£3.75 million. A record fee, my son.'

At that, I'd hold out my hand so they could pledge allegiance to Don Mark; at least, that's how I remember it.

This was a vital lesson. Always be sure of your source. On this, I knew I could go in all guns blazing. It was in *The Times*, which back then was as good as Fabrizio Romano. 'Have some of that, ya pricks.' Don't come crawling to me with your crocodile tears when you look like a prat. But it's no wonder we've all grown so cautious when it comes to transfer news. Not so long ago, it seemed Wesley Sneijder was spotted house-hunting in Cheshire every summer, ready for his big move to United. Those apparently in the know told us it was a sure thing . . . he must still be doing his medical.

In 1999, the *News of the World* even ran an exclusive story linking Liverpool with French superstar Didier Baptiste. There was one problem, though. Baptiste was a fictional character from the show *Dream Team*! This wasn't even April Fool's Day! This is the thing with transfer news. Any knobhead can make it up. We're all so desperate for good news that we lap it up, pass it on, then look like twats ourselves. Why do people do it? Let the story below be a lesson to you.

Like I said, in the 1990s, transfer news was hard to come by. If you didn't get it from a newspaper, your next best bet was teletext. For those of a younger age, teletext was like a really primitive version of the internet that you could access on your TV. I always remember the channel number of the football page: 302. It was my god. Every day, I'd scour it for transfer news. But there was something else advertised on teletext that was even better: the club line.

The club line was a law unto itself. This was the Wild West of transfer news. It would lure you in with some outrageous story, like 'Alex Ferguson to Manage Liverpool!' which would have you scrambling for your phone and dialling, all at the extortionate cost of £1.50 per minute. These were clever fuckers, though. They'd never get straight to the good stuff. They'd string it out with all sorts of shit, so by the time you got to the made-up nonsense that Sir Alex wasn't joining Liverpool, he'd just been spotted at a Bootleg Beatles concert, you were probably £50 down. Even though we knew it was all total bullshit, we still couldn't help ourselves. Did I ever succumb to the club line? Of course, I did. Who couldn't resist a story linking United to buying the entire Juventus team for 50 quid and a tube of Fruit Pastilles!? But after Mum went mental about the phone bill, I soon realised this wasn't a sustainable habit and went back to the apparently trusted journalists at the *Sun*, who would never dream of making up a transfer story to sell papers . . .

Wanting to test the system and have a bit of fun, one night my mate and I got drunk and decided to ring the United club line with an inside scoop. My mate told them that his mum worked in the canteen at Forest and all the talk was that Roy Keane was coming home. He'd fallen out with the head chef at United because his beans were too cold on his cooked breakfast and now he wanted to return to where it all started. Of course, this was total bullshit. It was also farcical. Even if Roy Keane was going to leave United, he would have had his pick of the world's best clubs. As if he'd go back to bloody Forest.

Despite this, the next day we clicked on the Forest and United club line pages and there it was. The lead bloody story. I have to tell you, though, it destroyed my faith in the system. I also felt very guilty. The big dogs at club line probably made a couple of grand from mugs ringing them up like drug addicts, hungry for their transfer news fix.

If you owned a club line back then, it was all consequence-free. Post some shit, pocket the money and ride off into the sunset. There's no chance of that today. If I post any sort of transfer story on Twitter, then within seconds, there are thousands of people writing comments, telling me I'm full of shit, and threatening to take my cat hostage unless I give up my source. For the last bloody time, that's not how it works. If I give up my source, do you think I'll ever get told anything again? Use your noggin! For fuck's sake.

Either way, this is all a vital lesson. Be sure of your bloody sources before you get too carried away. And don't get too excited, because remember, if it sounds too good to be true, it's probably just two drunk teenagers making up shite.

## EMBRACE THE ROLLERCOASTER

It's all fun and games when your club is linked to a player. It's like flirting with that girl you liked in school. You flutter your eyelashes, buy her a box of Matchmakers on Valentine's Day and hope she'll dance with you at the school disco. Sometimes, it all pays off, and you sign Robin van Persie from Arsenal and win the title. But usually, you're left standing alone, drinking Panda Pops, blue smeared all over your lips, watching on as the love of your life dances to 'I Will Always Love You' with the school bully.

'Are you crying, Mark?'

'No . . . just thinking of Eric Cantona.'

This is how transfer windows pan out for a lot of clubs. It's a rollercoaster of emotions. You have your eye on the prize, only for it to be snatched away at the last moment. Sometimes it's even worse than that. Rather than signing new players, you're just desperate to keep the ones you already have. You feel almost powerless when your star player is seemingly very open to some sunshine, paella and sangria in one of Europe's capital cities. Unless, that is, you're Andrei Kanchelskis.

After being a key player for United, Andrei decided he'd had enough of winning trophies and, in 1995, was lured to a relegation fight with Everton instead. At the time no one really understood his motivation to downgrade, especially when everyone at United was desperate to keep him. Conspiracy theories went into overdrive, with one in particular catching on: that the Russian mafia might have given Kanchelskis very little choice in the matter. When Igor from Moscow is (allegedly) hanging you over the edge of a balcony, trading Sir Alex Ferguson for Joe Royle doesn't seem so bad. Still, I bet he had to think twice about it.

'Hold on, Igor, how far is the drop? Maybe a broken leg isn't so bad . . .'

But not all transfers away from Manchester United can be explained by the Russian mob. No matter how much it hurts, sometimes you have to accept that a player wants to leave. So, let this story be a lesson to you. It's never as bad as it seems. Strap yourself in for the ride, and have faith that it'll all be alright in the end.

By 2003, David Beckham was England's poster boy. He wasn't called Golden Balls for nothing. I bloody loved Becks.

Who didn't? His last-minute free kick against Greece had sent England to the 2002 World Cup, while his performances during the 1999 treble-winning season were incredible. People forget, he finished second in the Ballon d'Or that year, just behind Rivaldo but ahead of Shevchenko, Batistuta and Figo. No one could cross a ball or take a free kick better than Beckham in his prime. He was so good with crosses vampires were terrified of him. Better still, he was one of our own. He'd come through United's academy and had been a United fan since he was a kid. To top it all, he was one cool bastard. We all wanted the bleached blond barnet, the skinhead, the mohican, though maybe not the braids – but still, he was a global phenomenon, a one-man marketing machine known all over the globe.

However, the rumour mill was rife that Becks wanted to go to Real Madrid. It's always those bastards, isn't it? And this was the era of the Galacticos, when Madrid signed a superstar every summer. Figo. Zidane. Ronaldo. In principle, it sounded great, but the rest of the team was made up of players who were like a gang of dogs trying to shag with ice skates on. It was like Whitney Houston in a duet with Jill Scott. It was more of a marketing project than a serious football club. I hated the thought of Beckham leaving. Like I said, he was one of our own. But he was a superstar, and becoming a Galactico made sense. After Sir Alex twatted a football boot in his face, it became pretty clear he'd reached the end of the road at Old

Trafford. By June, he was signing for Madrid, with a double fucking ponytail. The big sexy twat. It was a bloody calamity. I was gutted, but the prospect of his replacement allowed me to really let go.

At the time, United was linked with Ronaldinho. Yes, fucking please! I'll have some of that with some jam on top! A World Cup winner with Brazil just a year before, Ronaldinho was one of the best players in the world; *joga bonito* personified. Who cared about Becks when we'd soon have Ronaldinho doing the samba in front of the Stretford End. Thanks for the memories and all, Becks, but I was ready to drive him to Madrid myself. Adios, pal!

Every morning that summer, I raced to the local newsagent's and eagerly scoured the back pages for any slither of news. There was no doubt about it. Ronaldinho wanted out of PSG, and United was leading the chase. With Becks gone, the sacred number 7 shirt was ready and waiting for a more-than-worthy successor. Best. Robson. Cantona. Beckham. Ronaldinho. Magnificent! Get the Pringles out. We're having a party!

It seemed it was just a matter of time until it happened. I was so bloody excited. Some of my mates, who were fans of rival clubs, were so upset they would have made Anthony Martial look cheerful. It all made such perfect sense. One of the greatest players in the world was coming to the Theatre of

Dreams. But then it all went wrong . . . very, very fucking wrong.

One sunny day in July, I flicked through a pile of newspapers in the newsagent's, only to see Ronaldinho's cheeky face stare back from every back page. *This is it,* I thought. *Time to get your shirt ready, Mark. We're cooking now.* But when I picked up the newspaper, my face dropped, as if I was Lee Sharpe being caught at a house party by Sir Alex. Ronaldinho wasn't coming to United after all. Overnight, he had signed for Barcelona. The deal was already done and dusted. I actually shouted 'Oh fuck off,' in the shop.

*Barcelona!* I just couldn't grasp it. What was he thinking? You've got to remember; this was before the glory days of Pep. Hell, it was before Frank Rijkaard had whipped them into any sort of shape. In the summer of 2003, Barca was in disarray. The Louis van Gaal era had gone up in smoke. After finishing sixth in La Liga, Barca was a million miles away from the all-conquering tiki-taka side it would eventually become. I was seriously pissed off that we had somehow lost out to them. I'm sorry, Ronaldinho, you've made a right twat of yourself. Didn't he want to play with Eric Djemba-Djemba and Kleberson?

Things quickly went from bad to worse. Or so I thought. While I was trying to grasp the news that Ronaldinho wasn't coming to Old Trafford, we somehow still had to replace

Beckham. With his £25 million transfer fee burning a hole in our back pocket, I scrambled around in my head for who might still be a worthy replacement. Names such as Deco or Pavel Nedved were bandied about. Not quite as exciting as Ronaldinho but still bloody good. So, when the news broke that United had signed some unknown Portuguese kid called Ronaldo instead, I was furious.

If social media had been a thing back then, the videos would still be haunting me 20 years on. *Ronaldo! A pound-shop replica of the real Ronaldo . . . What a shambles of a clusterfuck . . . He's not fit to wear the shirt . . .* You get the picture. Truth is, barely any of us had any idea who Ronaldo was – not even *Championship Manager* fanatics, who could tell you all about Peru's reserve goalkeeper. Back then, there were no YouTube player reels that could make even Jordan Henderson look like prime Zidane. We were in the dark.

The first time most United fans might have known Ronaldo existed was during our pre-season game against Sporting Lisbon. The story goes that this young kid was so sensational that the likes of Gary Neville begged Sir Alex to sign him after the game. Sir Alex was already one step ahead of him. Quickly drafting a contract, Sir Alex refused to leave the stadium until the skinny, Pot-Noodle-headed teenager signed on the dotted line.

'Where do you think you're going?'

'Back home, to Lisbon.'

'Get in that fucking suitcase. You're going to Salford.'

'Yes, boss.'

Like I said, I was furious when I found out about this. It seemed ludicrous that we would replace David Beckham, a global superstar, with an unknown Portuguese kid. 'The board should resign', 'Fergie has lost the plot' . . . but it worked out pretty well, didn't it? After two consecutive Premier League titles, a European Cup and scoring 42 goals in 49 games, Ronaldo became the first United player to win the Ballon d'Or since George Best in 1968. Have that, Ronaldinho! (He might have won two La Ligas and a Champions League at Barca, but could he have done it on a wet and windy night in Stoke?)

This was an invaluable lesson. The transfer window is a rollercoaster. Your star players might leave. You might not get the signings you want. Get used to it. Hell, embrace it. What seems like a disaster can turn into one of the best things that has ever happened to your football club. Just think of Luis Suárez replacing Fernando Torres at Liverpool (let's not mention Andy Carroll) and Erling Haaland replacing Sergio Agüero at City. Spurs sold Harry Kane and are a much better side now he's left, while West Ham flogged Declan Rice and have kept chugging along.

Of course, sometimes it doesn't work out. When Mark Bosnich was signed to replace Peter Schmeichel, he turned up for his first day of training three hours late and overweight.

The less said about the rest of his time at United, the better. Still, when in doubt, it's probably best to remember the tale of Beckham, Ronaldinho and Ronaldo.

## BEING CHUFFED FOR MAN CITY

Someone call the police. Goldbridge has been kidnapped. He's saying he's chuffed for Man City. Remember the date. But it's true. Well, sort of. And you should be, too.

It's no secret that I'm a United fan. Common sense dictates that, more often than not, I'm going to follow and be far more interested and excited at any transfer news that involves United. Despite this, first and foremost, I consider myself a football fan. This means I want the Premier League to be the best in the world. I want all of the game's superstars to have played here at some point in their careers. I always think it's a real shame that the likes of Zidane, Messi and the Brazilian Ronaldo never played in the Premier League. So, if a club other than United brings a good player to the league, I'm still chuffed. I'd rather United had signed Haaland, but I still think it's great he plays in England, even if it is for those light blue wankers. Seriously though. It's a win-win. The standard of the league has improved, and that really should encourage United to bring in more top-quality players if we want to compete with the best.

This was particularly exciting in the nineties. Before 1994, foreign players were a real rarity in the Premier League. You might get the odd Eric Cantona or even Dwight Yorke and Peter Schmeichel, but we had always struggled to attract the really big-name players in their prime. Even back in the days when English clubs were dominating Europe, you never saw a Gerd Müller or Platini come here. Although Diego Maradona apparently came close to signing for Second Division Sheffield United in 1978 for £200,000. Imagine that! It'd be like Kylian Mbappé signing for Preston North End!

However, from the mid-1990s, things began to change. Jürgen Klinsmann signed for Spurs. Ruud Gullit signed for Chelsea. Dennis Bergkamp signed for Arsenal. The likes of Fabrizio Ravanelli and Juninho were soon looking bewildered when signing for Middlesbrough. Soon, nearly every club in the Premier League had signed a top foreign player. When Crystal Palace was relegated in 1998, the squad boasted Italian international Attilio Lombardo in its ranks. Teams like Leicester were signing Roberto Mancini. World Cup winner Youri Djorkaeff ended up in Bolton, while Christophe Dugarry was at Birmingham. There were, however, some clangers along the way as well.

Andrea Silenzi became the first Italian to play in England when he signed for Forest in 1995. After 20 games and just two goals, his contract was torn up. Dutchman Marco Boogers was even worse. After signing for West Ham in 1995 for £1 million, he lasted just four games, in one of which he was sent off for a horrific challenge on Gary Neville. Soon after, he disappeared to the Netherlands and was rumoured to be living in a caravan. Apparently Neville and his family holiday there every summer. Or as Gary calls it, a mini retirement. Transfer disasters like this might have been somewhat expected though. English clubs were dipping their toes into the foreign transfer market for the first time and were bound to get bitten. A bit like the first guy who jumped in the lake and discovered that piranhas exist. But the tale of Ali Dia is really something else. How the bloody hell did this even happen?

In 1996, reigning World Player of the Year George Weah gave Southampton manager Graeme Souness a ring. He told Souness that his cousin, Ali Dia, had been a very talented youngster at PSG and had just scored two goals for Senegal. He was sure he could do a job in the Premier League, and Souness should give him a trial. Now, as if *any* of this sounds real. Yet somehow, Souness took the bait, not for one minute checking if any of this was actually true. Which is surprising from someone who's 'Played the Game'.

When Dia arrived for his trial, Souness barely saw him play. He was too preoccupied dealing with an injury crisis before Southampton's game with Leeds. Down to the bare bones, and still going on George Weah's word, Souness decided to put Dia on the bench. It gets even funnier.

In the 32nd minute, disaster struck. Matt Le Tissier got injured and had to come off. Souness duly sent Dia on in his place. As you can imagine, he was as useful as a marzipan dildo. After 53 minutes, Souness realised he was looking like a right twat and gave him the hook. By then, it probably dawned on him that the phone call hadn't been from George Weah, and Ali Dia wasn't some hot prospect. He was actually a 31-year-old university student who had played a bit of non-league football. Dear. Dear. Dear . . . Bloody funny, though.

So, the foreign invasion didn't always work out for every-one, but it still took the Premier League to another level. There were far more hits than shits. Best of all, as far as I was concerned, it also made United improve along with it. Just think how hard Arsenal and Arsène Wenger pushed United with a team made up of the likes of Petit, Vieira, Overmars and Bergkamp. I hated them, but that was a serious team. We had to dramatically improve if we were going to compete. Just as Messi and Ronaldo had to raise their games against each other, so did Keane when he faced Vieira. Without the foreign influence on Arsenal and their star players, I'm certain that United would not have won the Champions League in 1999. It made us raise our level. Before the foreign invasion, we had struggled in Europe. Yet now we were playing against the best foreign players in the Premier League on a weekly basis. If we could win the Premier League against that lot, we'd also stand a better chance in Europe.

That's how I see it with City today. It bloody stings when they're signing good players and winning everything in sight. But that's the level. If we want to be the best in Europe again, then we have to topple City. Like an overconfident cat, they're staring us right in the eyes, shitting right on our doorstep. We know what we have to do to compete at the top table. Otherwise, it's good night Vienna. And good night, Brighton and Brentford, while we're at it.

So, there's no point in being envious of other teams signing good players. Enjoy the ride, embrace the best footballers playing in the Premier League, and hope it forces your team to meet the challenge.

## BIG-NAME SIGNINGS

There's nothing like a big-name signing to get the pulse racing. Get the caviar and champagne out. Tell your partner to put their best lingerie on and turn out the lights. Shit is about to go down.

If your club is going to spend tens of millions of pounds on a player, surely the execs have done their homework. And you can see, with your own God-given eyes, that the player is bloody good. This isn't some random bloke with a good YouTube reel who you're taking a punt on. This is the real bloody deal. But just chill your boots. I don't want to be a grump but let's just take a moment to recap why big-name players aren't always all they're cracked up to be.

In 2021, Ronaldo might have been in his mid-thirties, but he was coming off another shit-hot season at Juventus. Scoring 29 league goals, he was also the top scorer in Italy. Something had gone wrong somewhere, though, and he wanted out. Better yet, he was available for just £12.5 million. However, to every United fan's horror, it seemed like he was all set to join Pep at Man City. Then, Sir Alex and Agent Rio muscled in. I imagine their conversation with Ronaldo was like the scene in *Casino Royale* when Mads Mikkelsen has Daniel Craig strapped naked to a chair and threatens to electrocute his balls.

'But I want to play for one of the best managers and teams in Europe.'

Sir Alex nods his head to Agent Rio.

ZAP!!!!

'FFS, Rio! Alright, I'll play for Ole Gunnar Solskjaer and with Jesse Lingard.'

A pat on the back. 'Well done, son. You've made the right choice.'

At this, City were out of the race. The prodigal son was returning home after all. From out of nowhere, we had suddenly re-signed one of our greatest players. 'Walking in a Goldbridge wonderland!' It all went well for a little bit. In his first season, he scored 24 goals in all competitions. This was a good return, especially as he did this while playing in one of the worst United teams in living memory. Then it all went very, very wrong . . . loss of form, change of manager, tantrums, tiaras, Piers Morgan. Talk about a disaster. Within 18 months he was slamming the door behind him on his way to Saudi Arabia. Why, Ronnie? Why?

Ronaldo isn't an isolated incident, at least not as far as United is concerned. Seriously, our transfer team is as useful as an ashtray on a motorbike. What time is it, Mr Wolf? It's bloody dinner time when the United transfer team rolls into town. Is it a car? Is it a plane? No, it's Ed Woodward and his gang of prats. This goes way back as well.

One of the transfers I was most excited about was in 2001, when United signed Argentina's Juan Sebastián Verón for £28.1 million. He was a genuine superstar for club and country. Technically, he could do it all. With that right boot of his, he could peel a chocolate orange, but it seemed that the Premier League was too fast and physical for him. In the end, we were playing Phil Neville in midfield ahead of him. That still doesn't sound right to me. To the younger reader this would be like dropping Virgil van Dijk for Eric Dier.

Then, in 2015, we signed a big slab of Germany's finest in Bastian Schweinsteiger. We'd been linked to him for years. He just seemed the perfect fit for what we needed. A no-nonsense central midfielder who could do everything well and was also a leader, the heir to Keane's vacated throne. I also liked the fact that he was German. We always admire the Germans for their winning mentality, and he was the ultimate example. At Bayern Munich, he'd won eight league titles and the Champions League, and had also won the World Cup in 2014. It therefore made sense to get one of Germany's renowned winners into a United team that was more like prime Stoke than prime Barcelona. But things didn't really work out for Bastian at Old Trafford. Looking back, it should have been obvious we were having our tummies tickled before being told to roll over. A team like Bayern Munich isn't going to happily sell one of German football's superstars unless that player is past it. Fair play to Bastian; you can't accuse him of not trying, but it was like he was running through porridge. In fact, you could describe his time at United as constipation football. Lots of pain and effort to ultimately deliver a shitshow!

At least Schweinsteiger wanted to be at Old Trafford and gave it his best. You can't say the same for old whiny-face Ángel Di María. Schweinsteiger was set for the glue factory when he signed for United, but Di María was in his prime. He was just 26 years old, at the top of the assists chart in Spain and had won the Player of the Match award in the Champions League final for Madrid. Yet, for the grand sum of £59.7 million and £280,000 a week, he stunk the place out. Someone call the police. I'd like to report a robbery. My fucking days. It was like he had salmon for feet and candyfloss for a heart.

After just 27 underwhelming games and 3 goals, he was packed off to PSG. Get your coat and your shoes, Ángel, and piss off.

Perhaps the all-time clusterfuck where United are concerned, though, is Alexis Sánchez. I still can't work out how this transfer went so badly wrong. He'd been a bloody superstar for Arsenal, one of the best players in the league – you might even say world-class – and he was only 30 years old. Everyone was buzzing when we snatched him away from Man City, who were waving a four-and-a-half-year deal and a load of trophies in his face. Sure, his wage demands were steep, coming in at over £400,000 a week, but surely he would be worth it. Was he fuck! It was a bloody disaster. United got screwed so much on this deal we might as well have a United transfer category on Pornhub. Piano promo videos are all well and fucking good, but after three goals in one-and-a-half underwhelming seasons we'd have been better off signing Elton John. We loaned him to Inter (paying half his salary as well) and of course he won Serie A! I'm still waiting for Jeremy Beadle to jump out at me.

So, just take a tip from Uncle Mark. Don't get seduced by reputation and a fancy name. Remember, some of the best players your club has ever signed have likely been cheap and relatively unknown. Some of the United greats certainly fall into this category. Take Ole Gunnar Solskjaer, for example.

In 1996, the Baby-faced Assassin was signed for £1.5 million from Norwegian club Molde. No one thought anything of it. He looked like a child who'd won a day out at Old Trafford. There was no way he would cut it in the Premier League. A grand total of 126 goals in 366 games later, including the winner in the Champions League final, tells a very different story. Of those goals, 26 were off the bench, four of which he scored in just 12 minutes against Nottingham Forest, whose defenders played like a bunch of Morris dancers playing hide and seek with a hungry lion. Jingle bells everywhere.

Every club can boast a signing like this. At one point, it seemed Arsenal were plucking them out of the bag every single summer. Nicolas Anelka was unknown when he signed for £500,000 in 1997. Two years later, he'd won the double and joined Real Madrid for £24 million. Then, there was Patrick Vieira, Emmanuel Petit and Freddie Ljungberg, to name just a few.

Man City might have splashed the cash in recent years and then some, but perhaps the most vital player in the club's history was one they signed on the cheap. In 2008, Vincent Kompany signed from Hamburg for just £6 million. He soon became club captain and led City to four Premier League titles, including their first since 1968. Typically, United had looked to sign him in 2004, but bought Gabriel Heinze instead. 'If I speak . . .'

Then there's Leicester City, who turned signing unknown prospects into an art form. In 2012, they picked up 25-year-old Jamie Vardy for £1 million from non-league Fleetwood

Town. Two years later, Riyad Mahrez signed for £450,000 from Ligue 2 club Le Havre, where he'd scored just 6 goals in 60 games. A year later, N'Golo Kanté arrived from Caen for £5.6 million. No one paid any attention to these arrivals. Not even Leicester fans were enthused. But my fucking days, did they deliver. With those three in tandem, Leicester improbably won the Premier League in 2016. In doing so, Vardy scored 24 league goals, including scoring in 11 consecutive games. Mahrez was just as influential, scoring 17 league goals and winning the Professional Footballers' Association (PFA) Players' Player of the Year award. However, Kanté was the glue that held the team together. While he topped the league's defensive stats, he also drove the team forward, turning defence into attack. He was like two players in one. It's no exaggeration to say he was one of the best midfielders the league has ever seen.

Like I said, don't get too carried away with your big-name signings. Most of them are as useful as nipples on Christian Bale's Batsuit. At the same time, give your unknowns a chance. You might just have unearthed the next Kanté.

## NEW BOY BLUES

Remember that feeling you have on your first day at a new job? You probably tuck your shirt into your pants, spill coffee over your boss and accidentally tell your best rude joke to the resident Bible-basher. So, imagine your first day at work in a new country, with 70,000 people in the stadium watching your every move and millions more watching on TV. You're going to shit your pants, aren't you, so I don't know why we expect footballers in their twenties to be any different. Cut them some slack. Don't kick them in the bin straight away. There's still hope you haven't signed a complete clown. Hop into a DeLorean with me and take a trip back to January 2006 to see what I'm talking about.

At the time, United was facing a defensive crisis. In his wisdom, Sir Alex signed Patrice Evra and Nemanja Vidić for a grand total of £12.5 million. Big money, certainly, to spend in January. But Sir Alex is rarely wrong in the transfer market. Therefore, expectations were sky-high for these two to save our season. Their first few weeks, however, were a fucking calamity. Evra was so bad that he was hauled off at half-time on his debut. Vidić's first game wasn't much better, as he was part of a defence that shipped four goals to Blackburn! Both defended like an Easter egg on a hot day, melting away under the slightest pressure.

Even their teammates weren't having them. Paul Scholes has since admitted that the United players were 'concerned' by how poor the two new boys were. That's an understatement, Scholesy. On the *Filthy @ Five* podcast, Rio Ferdinand revealed a conversation he had with Wayne Rooney about the pair:

I remember after one session, me and Wazza were walking around. He said, 'Who the fuck is this guy?' He was terrible. Vidić and Evra signed in the same window and he [Rooney] was going: 'The manager has fucked it, he's messed up, I don't know what's going on with the recruitment.'

Granted, Vidić and Evra were about as intimidating as a butterfly's fart when they first joined. However, by 2008, both were key players in United's European Cup win. In the end they were so good they'd both probably feature in most conversations about the greatest full-back and centre back in Premier League history.

Plenty of other players have also gone on to flourish after sticky starts. Dennis Bergkamp didn't score in his first seven league games for Arsenal after arriving for a club record £7.5 million from Inter Milan. David de Gea was so bad in his first few games at United that he was dropped for Anders Lindegaard. Didier Drogba scored just ten goals in his first season at Chelsea. Future Ballon d'Or winner Luka Modric was heralded as the worst signing of the season after arriving at Madrid. All of them were mocked and derided, but with a little bit of patience, they came good and then some.

Sadly, not everyone can transform into a butterfly. For every Vidić and Evra, a team has a bag of shit, or an El Hadji Diouf, Sean Dundee, Jimmy Carter, Iago Aspas, István Kozma,

Andriy Voronin, Torben Piechnik or Alberto Aquilani. What a fucking list that is. I'm sorry, Liverpool fans, I really am, but I'll let you have Van Dijk. As far as Neil Warnock was concerned, he was no better than Sol Bamba, so Jürgen Klopp worked wonders there . . .

## NEVER FALL IN LOVE WITH A LOAN PLAYER

Everyone has their favourite player at their club. Usually, they're tucked away on a long-term contract so you can relax. It's safe to fall in love with them. Enjoy the first flourish of romance, then settle down for a binge session on Netflix in your jogging bottoms, eating takeaways on your laps.

'Fancy a foot rub, Bruno?'

'Thanks, Mark; pass me the Twiglets while you're at it.'

'God, I love you.'

It's all very safe. Neither of you is going anywhere, even if things get a bit rocky. You're Daniel Levy. They're Harry Kane. You just have to grin and bear it. You've got their balls in a vice, and they know it. However, don't get too comfortable. There are some players representing your club who you have to guard your heart against.

In modern football, it's accepted that in most seasons, your team might sign a loan player or two. This can happen for a variety of reasons. On the one hand, smaller clubs are usually quite happy to take an up-and-coming youngster from a bigger club on loan. In recent years, we've seen the likes of Conor Gallagher at Palace and Mason Mount at Derby – even Harry Kane did the loan rounds, representing Leyton Orient, Norwich, Millwall and Leicester. It's a win-win for everyone. On the other hand, there are big-money signings who just haven't worked out, and a potential new club wants to try before they buy. Just look at Spurs letting everyone have a sniff of their record signing Tanguy Ndombélé. Alternatively, you might be a big club with crap owners and no transfer strategy. Breathe, Mark. Breathe. Nice and slow . . .

Either way, loans can often be positive for the player, the parent club and the club that's loaning them. Everyone's bloody happy with their lot. Nice to see you. To see you, nice. But they don't factor the fans into this. We're the ones who get hurt the most. We need to protect ourselves from the heartless scourge of the loan player before we find ourselves banging on the players' G-Wagon doors as they exit the car park, begging them to take us back.

Loan players are flings and need to be treated as such. Sordid little rendezvous. They're only going to be with you for a brief period of time. No matter how much you want the relationship to continue, there will be no end-of-film airport scene where you rush to the gate and they collapse into your arms and agree to stay. 'Plymouth! You complete me.' Just accept that the following season, you'll see your hero in another club's shirt, kissing the badge. Bastards. It's going to hurt more than a spiky butt plug.

Over the years, United has made a right twat of itself in the loan market. To be honest, it's been hard to fall in love with most of the players we've signed. The mere mention of some of these names should come with a trigger warning for some United fans.

In December 1995, United had an injury crisis at the back. Gary Pallister, Steve Bruce and David May were all facing a spell on the sidelines, but Sir Alex didn't want to waste money on signing a replacement. He just needed a short-term solution. This is how William Prunier, a journeyman centre back from Bordeaux, came to play for Manchester United. And it was a total fucking disaster.

In his second appearance, Prunier faced a struggling Spurs team at White Hart Lane. This was usually meat and drink for the mighty United. In the words of Roy Keane, 'Lads, it's Spurs.' Yet United lost the game by four bastard goals to one, with Chris Armstrong running Prunier ragged. Chris fucking Armstrong! It was no surprise that Prunier didn't appear for the club again, even with an injury crisis. Although Prunier does claim Ferguson still offered him a three-year deal. Really, William? He should go for a pint with my mate John. He's a complete full-of-shit fantasist too. Last week he told us Margot Robbie had slipped into his DMs on Insta and invited him round for a lasagne and a shag.

There have been a few more loan players through the door at Old Trafford since, with no danger of any emotional attachment. Goalkeeper Andy Goram only arrived after telling Alex Ferguson to 'Fuck off', thinking it was a prank call by Ally McCoist. That's how ludicrous it seemed to the player, so imagine what the fans thought of it. In recent years, we've also sampled the joys of Odion Ighalo and Wout Weghorst. There was never any danger of falling in love with them. I'd rather date roadkill. They were cheapskate signings and performed exactly how we expected. Crap at best. The only saving grace was that they were clearly stunned and delighted to be at a club like Manchester United. Still, watching balls bounce off Weghorst like he was a trampoline for half a season wasn't much fun. 'Oh, but he presses really well . . .' Go buy a fucking iron then. Seriously. However, not all of our loan signings have been from the reject section in Poundland.

On transfer deadline day in 2014, United signed Radamel Falcao on loan from Monaco. This was a real thoroughbred. I was fully prepared to fall head over heels in love with the Colombian superstar with the granite chin and flowing locks. Sure, he was just returning from a bad knee injury, but before that, he'd been one of the best players in Europe. His hat-trick for Atlético Madrid against Chelsea in the Super Cup was only two years before, and he was still only 28 years old. I was sure we'd soon get him back to his best at United. And if we did, then we'd probably sign him. Taking all that into account, I was ready to greet him at the airport with a kiss and a bunch of roses. 'I'm all yours, Radamel; take me to Rome.' We're walking on bloody sunshine. However, he was rustier than a bike left in the pouring rain for a year. Across 29 appearances, Falcao scored just 4 goals. By the end of his spell at Old Trafford, he was the world's best fertiliser, spreading shit all over the pitch. Things didn't get much better for him the following season on loan at Chelsea, where he scored once in 12 appearances. However, by 2017, he finally returned to form at his parent club, Monaco, banging in 30 goals in 43 games as he helped them win the French title. You just hate to be bloody right sometimes.

There is one loan signing, however, who did impress, and also broke my heart. Super Swede Henrik Larsson had enjoyed a glittering career, banging in goals for Celtic, Barcelona and Sweden. He was so clinical he could perform open-heart surgery on an ant. After winning the Champions League with Barcelona in 2006, he decided to return to his hometown club, Helsingborg. However, the Swedish league was over by December, and it was probably a bit shit, so by January he found himself twiddling his thumbs, dreaming of a final fling at the big time. At the time United was down to the bare bones in the forward department, with only Wayne Rooney and Louis Saha being fit. The solution was staring everyone in the face. Get yourself to Manchester, Henrik. You've pulled.

I tried not to get carried away. I knew Larsson's best days were behind him, and his stint in Manchester would only last a few weeks before he returned to Sweden. Sometimes, though, you can't help yourself. The United side at the time wasn't one of Sir Alex's finest vintages. We were going through a transitional stage, eventually blossoming into the Champions League-winning team of 2008. Yet for a few seasons prior, we weren't quite at it. So, when Larsson proved he was still a top-class player, it made it hard to let go.

In 13 games at United, he scored 3 goals, including the winner in a Champions League match against Lille. It doesn't sound fantastic, but his presence lifted the team and made everyone raise their game. Suddenly, there was a buzz around Old Trafford again. And then, just like a Paul Daniels magic trick, he was gone in a puff of smoke. The love affair lasted just eight weeks. While he was clearly tempted to stay, he kept his promise to Helsingborg and reported back for the start of the Swedish season. This sense of loyalty only made me love him more. It all made me sad, though. There was a sense of what might have been, not only at him not extending his loan but having not signed him earlier in his career. With Larsson returning to Sweden, we were stuck with just Saha up front to support Rooney. With Saha's injury record, this was a bit like asking a breadstick to support a bowl of oranges. Unfortunately, Saha always snapped under pressure.

Larsson had lured me in and spat me out. I swore not to make the same mistake again, but sometimes we can't help ourselves. Spare yourself the heartbreak. Respect your loan players. Cheer for them. But never, ever fall in love with them. Henrik, we'll always have Watford.

# 3

# THE JOY OF PRE-SEASON

Another season is over. There's no international tournament. Nothing to get the juices flowing at all. For a time, you're lost, forced to confront the real world. Saturday afternoons are suddenly a black void. What are you supposed to do with yourself? Like plenty of others, you find yourself eating meatballs at IKEA, observing other bewildered fans in the same predicament. Is this what a real person does? How did you even get here? Ludicrous. But there is some hope: pre-season.

Now, I was once like you. Pre-season was a chore, nothing more than a series of meaningless football matches where players try to find some fitness and form, and Phil Jones finally gets some game time. If he's fit, that is. But then I saw the light. Pre-season is football on meth. Once you can accept this, then the fun really begins. Pull up a seat and let me convert you into a pre-season ultra.

## PRE-SEASON PIRLO

Now, I learned this the hard way. There's no point in wasting your time or energy on regular first-team players in pre-season. It'll only lead to disappointment. Most aren't that bothered or are just trying to find their touch. Some, like Scott McTominay, are still trying to find it. Forget your big-name stars. They're not arsed. Put them in the bin for the summer. Embrace your fringe players instead.

In pre-season, the fringe player will be doing everything to impress. They've been like a fly in a jam jar for months, waiting for their chance to be released into the wild. So, when they come up against Torquay's reserve full-back, they're utterly fucking ruthless. They don't care if these guys have families. For them, they're just a meme waiting to happen.

In recent years United have had a few youngsters who have looked the bollocks in pre-season. Tahith Chong looked like a superstar in the making in 2019 when he tore Inter a new one. Zidane Iqbal was immense in 2021 and Jesse Lingard was notorious for turning up to pre-season ripped like Cristiano Ronaldo and playing like Messi on fastplay. But perhaps my favourite pre-season wonder is Andreas Pereira. It makes me all misty-eyed, this one. In 2015, he was so good the fans even nicknamed him 'Pre-Season Pirlo'.

If he wasn't scoring bangers against the mighty San Jose Earthquakes, he was running through Wigan like Imodium Plus. There he was, on both wings, as a number 10, and even in central midfield. Along with some outrageous flicks and tricks, there was a burst of pace to go with it, as well as passes being switched all over the pitch. I bloody loved him. I'd happily stay up until the middle of the night to watch him give those boys from San Jose a whipping. When United were linked to James Rodríguez, I even said there was no point in signing him. We already had Pereira.

Sadly, that was as good as it got for our 'Pre-Season Pirlo'. While he made 45 sporadic first-team appearances over eight seasons, he never looked the same as in pre-season. After a few loan moves, he eventually signed for Fulham for £10 million. He's still a good player, but never hit the heights we had all hoped for.

That's the purpose of a 'Pre-Season Pirlo', though. You need to accept that these players are for pre-season only. For them and you, that's as good as it's ever going to get. And that's fine. They more than serve their purpose in lighting up otherwise dull and pointless pre-season games. In my eyes, for these players, the real season is pre-season. Then they can rest and be in prime shape for the following pre-season when they can pull on a first-team shirt and cook again.

So, join in the fun. Get yourself a shirt that you only wear during pre-season. Get a fringe player's name and number printed on the back, and then, for the next six weeks, make your Pre-Season Pirlo a god.

## THE MAGIC OF PRE-SEASON

Everyone bloody loves a big upset in the Cup. Watching an underdog make a twat out of one of the big boys is one of the great thrills in football. Yet why do people only talk about the magic of the Cup? This sort of magic is on display every pre-season. And there are not only giant-killings galore but also fixtures you'd normally have no chance of seeing. Just consider some of these.

In 2019 Accrington Stanley beat ten-time French champions Marseille, while in 2018 Walsall beat Ajax 2–0. In 2023 Aldershot Town even beat Chelsea 3–1 and then trolled them on social media, calling them a 'mid-table Premier League side'. Magic. Stick that up your King's Road.

Of course, the bigger teams might not be fielding a full-strength side, but most don't in cup competitions either and everyone still gets their knickers in a twist if they lose. Besides, no matter what team they put out, everyone still goes into these games thinking the big dogs will win.

For many of the underdogs, this might be their only chance to ever play against a big team. This is their cup final. Some players will take a pre-season game like this far more seriously than any league game they'll play. Just look at Arsenal's pre-season clash with Barcelona in 2023. Those plucky underdogs ran their hearts out to beat the Spanish champions 5–3. Even Xavi said they'd played like it was the Champions League final.

In these games, there's something wonderful about watching an undercooked, half-arsed Premier League footballer being chased and kicked around the pitch, not having a clue what's going on. The crowd love it as well. Just like the players, this is a big game for them. The attendance might even be the biggest of the season. Best of all, the sun is usually shining. You get to sit back in your shorts and T-shirt and watch your team humiliate a giant. Drink it in. You can stuff the cup games, especially when they're in the middle of January and bloody freezing.

In the FA Cup or the EFL Cup, a giant-killing might happen once or twice a season. Yet it's a frequent occurrence in pre-season, so enjoy the chance to watch the giants get their pants pulled down. And if you're one of those giants, take some solace in it. Many a title-winning season has been built on the back of a horrific pre-season result. Take Liverpool. Please, take them. But seriously, in 2019, they were winless over four pre-season games, culminating in losing 3–0 to Napoli. It didn't matter though. They still went on to win their first league title in 30 years.

## WHEN TEAMS GO NUCLEAR

Just as good as any underdog upset is a giant coming to town and going full Ivan Drago from *Rocky IV*. 'If he dies. He dies.' Some of these games are against teams that are not much better than Sunday League sides. Still, they show no mercy. You mess with the big boys; this is what you'll get, ya little squirt.

As I said above, these fixtures are like a cup final for most of these teams. While it's glorious when they pull off an upset, there's also something satisfying about watching a group of guys give absolutely everything and still get humiliated when up against world-class footballers. These results aren't the sort of drubbings you might get in your standard cup game. These are your sex videos released on the internet – total and utter humiliation – with scorelines well into double figures, and even then only because in the second half the giants are too busy posing for selfies with fans mid-match.

For the last few pre-seasons, German giant Bayern Munich has taken on the amateur side FC Rottach-Egern. Not once has there been a sniff of a giant-killing. In 2019 Munich won the match 23–0, averaging a goal every four minutes. In 2023, knowing the calibre of the opposition, Bayern's players still didn't give a flying toss, this time putting 27 goals past them. The score was 18–0 at half-time! Four players scored three goals or more. You fucking asked for this, Rottach-Egern, and now you're gonna get it. Pass us the lube, it's time for another screwing. You almost wonder what anyone gets out of this, but every single year the fans turn up to watch their players get their arses handed to them on a silver platter by Germany's finest.

This type of pre-season massacre is far from an isolated incident. If you keep your eyes peeled, you'll see scores like this during most summers. In 2018 Everton destroyed Austrian amateurs ATV Irdning 22–0, while in 2023 Serie A's Sassuolo hammered Real Vicenza 22–0, with five players scoring hat-tricks. International teams also get in on the act too. In 1988 an England team featuring Gary Lineker, Bryan Robson, John Barnes, Peter Beardsley, Glenn Hoddle and Chris Waddle beat Aylesbury United 7–0. In the run-up to Euro 96, the Czech Republic tore apart non-league Bamber Bridge 9–1, with Karel Poborsky, Pavel Nedved, Patrik Berger and Vladimir Smicer all getting on the scoresheet.

It's not just the scorelines that make these games worth watching. In the final 30 minutes of these friendlies, piss-taking becomes an art form. You get to watch the top teams pass the ball between each other 100–200 times while the puffing and panting semi-pros are on the verge of a heart attack, never getting close to the ball. It's like being at the pub watching my mate John looking for his message from Margot. He'll never find it but it's great watching him squirm.

At the end of the day, everyone still goes home happy. The smaller team has made some decent money and their players have had a chance to share the pitch with their heroes. The players in the bigger team have also got some match fitness and had a bloody good laugh, which is always good for morale. When your striker has scored ten in the first game of pre-season, it can only be good for confidence. It must be like playing against Harry Maguire every week. Best of all, us fans get to see just why these players earn the big bucks compared to schmucks like us.

## EMBRACE THE CRAZY

Giant-killings and humiliations are expected in pre-season, but pre-season games can also turn football on its head. Anything can happen. It's like a funhouse mirror at the fairground. All rules and normality go out of the window. It's a plethora of insanity you'd never get during the regular season. Just check out some of this mind-boggling lunacy.

These days, the Premier League's top sides spend a lot of pre-season playing exhibition games abroad. In recent years, Man United has played in the United States, Australia and Asia. Not everyone is a fan of this, but it certainly beats the likes of the Dallas Tornado's 1967 pre-season tour, which took place in Vietnam in the middle of the war! Not only did they lose 26 of their 32 games, but they were also regularly attacked and had to eventually fuck off back home. It's like the Glazers organising a pre-season tour in Liverpool. Let's not give them any ideas . . .

Most of these games are against the respective country's best league sides. That's all well and good, but what really gets my blood pumping is when a league decides to put together an all-star team. These all-star teams are made up of the best players that the league has to offer, no matter their nationality. For instance, in 2019 DC United's Wayne Rooney lined up for the MLS All-Stars against Atlético Madrid. How good does that sound? Well, in pre-season, this is just par for the course.

What's even better is when a Premier League team absolutely pumps an all-star team, like in the summer of 2023, when Arsenal beat the MLS side 5–0. This was also in the middle of the American league's season, so all their players were fully fit and ready to go. I love watching any Premier League side give these all-star teams a lesson in humiliation. Taste our dominance, you big pricks. Suck on some of that. Who are ya? Who are ya?

Like I said, pre-season isn't your run-of-the-mill beans on toast. It's a Bacon Double Cheeseburger meal with halloumi fries. During pre-season, the players know they can afford to let off a little steam. Mario Balotelli pushed the boundaries at the best of times, but even he knew to treat league games with a little respect. This didn't apply in pre-season, though, where Mario could fuck around to his heart's content. Take Man City's pre-season game with the LA Galaxy in 2011.

In the 28th minute, Mario was put clean through on goal. Rather than slot the ball past the keeper, as he would in a game of any consequence, he instead decided to do a 180 back-heel and kick the ball out of play. It was jaw-dropping stuff. His manager, Roberto Mancini, certainly wasn't pleased, hauling him off straight away for not showing the game any respect. For me, Mancini got this one wrong. This was precisely what pre-season is all about. If you want to watch proper football, then wait until the season begins, you big boring prat. Pre-season is all about embracing the madness, and Super Mario knew this better than anyone. And anyway, who is Mancini to talk? He left the Italian national team job to manage in Saudi. That's literally taking the piss.

Unlike Mancini, there are some managers who totally understand what a friendly game is all about. In 1996 the Welsh national team, managed by 50-year-old Bobby Gould, took on the mighty Cwmbrân Town. With a team featuring Ryan Giggs, Mark Hughes and Gary Speed, it was no surprise that with half an hour to go, the national side were 5–0 up. By this stage, Gould had ants in his pants. It didn't matter that this was meant to be a game to prepare his players for a European qualification match. Gould also wanted to get in on the action, so subbed himself on and got on the end of a Ryan Giggs cross to score the sixth and final goal.

Harry Redknapp was another manager who respected the madness of pre-season. When West Ham took on Oxford City in 1994, 34-year-old Lee Chapman was toiling desperately up front for the Hammers. Still, it was a pre-season game, so he can be forgiven if he wasn't at full throttle. Apparently, this wasn't good enough for West Ham fan Steve Davies, who was sat behind the dugout. He proceeded to give Chapman a barrage of abuse for most of the first half, complaining loudly every time he touched the ball. 'Chapman, you're a fucking donkey.' You get the idea.

By half-time, Redknapp had had enough. Turning to confront Davies, he told him, 'You think you can do better, do you?' Davies told him he could, so Harry decided to take up the challenge. Handing Davies a kit and some boots, Harry took Chapman off and put Davies up front in his place. Unbelievably, he scored! Just imagine how Chapman felt. Absolute devastation. But this is what pre-season is all about.

Yet, some of the best things about pre-season don't even happen during the actual games. Take the MLS, which has always been a bit out there. When the league started in 1996, any games that ended in a draw were decided by a player from each team running with the ball from the halfway line to try and score a one-on-one. While that rule was eventually scrapped, the MLS is still happy to try some crazy stuff out. And what better time to do it than a pre-season game against a top Premier League team in front of a national television audience.

The MLS All-Star Skills Challenge sees players from each team having to complete a number of skills against each other. There are regular challenges like shooting, passing, volleying and even hitting the crossbar, but our crazy Yankee friends also introduced 'goalie wars'. This sees the two rival keepers face each other in goals placed about 20 yards apart and then doing whatever they like to score. It's total insanity. You can throw, thunderbastard or volley the ball however you like. Pull faces. Call out insults. All that matters is you somehow put the ball in the net.

Watching top players perform challenges like this when the pressure is off is usually a humbling experience. They get to put on a show, displaying the full range of their technique and repertoire, doing things they would never think of doing in a game. They might pull off bicycle kicks or, better still, scorpion kicks. No one will complain if they don't take it too seriously. But things get even better when a supposed top player freezes with the spotlight on him. Suddenly, he can't even do the basics. This is what happened to poor Kai Havertz during the MLS All-Star volley challenge in 2023.

After signing for Arsenal from Chelsea for £65 million just two weeks before, Arsenal fans watched in horror as their marquee signing proceeded to sky ball after ball over the bar. It was a horror show. Total humiliation and no place to hide. He missed all 14 shots and was the first player in MLS All-Star challenge history to get a score of zero. By the end, his confidence was shot, and it wasn't like he had a lot to begin with anyway. Still, watching a multimillion-pound footballer reduced to being no better than your average fan made for stellar pre-season entertainment.

I hope that, after reading this, I've managed to win you round. Pre-season isn't the appetiser before the big feast. It's a hog roast all by itself. Learn to embrace it in all of its glory.

# 4

# MATCH DAY

It was March 1989. Manchester United were playing Forest in the quarter-finals of the FA Cup. As it was close to my birthday, my dad got us some tickets. It was going to be my first trip to Old Trafford. I was bloody buzzing, but en route it almost ended in total humiliation.

'Dad, I need a wee.'

Dad turns to me in the back of his car, then looks at the traffic snaking ahead of us, leading to Old Trafford.

'You'll have to hold it.'

I squirm in my seat.

'I can't. I really need to go.'

Dad looks around as if a bog will magically appear in Manchester's industrial heartlands.

'There's nowhere to go, Mark.'

I grimace. Tap my feet. Bite my cheeks. Let out a little squeal. I can feel the urine pushing its way out of my bladder.

I'm about to give birth to a puddle of piss. Finally, there's nowhere left to go other than to accept my fate.

'I'm going to wet myself! I'm going to wet myself!'

Dad frantically looks around. I can sense his dilemma. The car isn't moving. There isn't a toilet in sight, nor even a bottle to wee in. Finally, his eyes set on something. He points across the road.

'Get out and go in that alley over there.'

I don't think to ask any questions. Throwing open the car door, I run across the traffic, dart into the alleyway, and pull my trousers down just as a torrent of piss explodes against the wall. The relief is instant. And I can't stop pissing. But why would you want to when pissing feels this good? You find a mark on the wall and hose that down while you're at it. Bang! Have some of that piss, ya prick. Fireman Mark and his big hose have saved the day again. A good piss and cleaning the wall while you're at it. That's what winning's made of.

With the fun at an end, I pull my pants up and look towards the car. The piss euphoria is over as reality bites and I see hundreds of brake lights flash red in the drizzle. In a panic, I look around. My dad's car is nowhere to be seen. I'm in a strange city, buildings towering over me, floods of strangers barging past. Shit.

The craziest thoughts flood my brain. I'm homeless. This is it. The streets are my home now. I'll have to toughen up. I'm like the kids in *Moonwalker*. Where are Michael Jackson and Bubbles when you need them? In fact, scrub that, I'd rather be homeless.

Just as I'm getting used to the idea of a pet rat and life in a bin, I hear a voice shout out over the hum of traffic. 'Mark! Mark!' I look up. Dad is about 50 yards ahead, standing by his car, waving frantically. I was saved, but deep down, I'd always know how Jesse Lingard felt after leaving Forest. Lost. Alone. Unwanted. My best life behind me.

For my first trip to Old Trafford, I remember little about the game other than Forest won. Of course they did. Start as you mean to go on, United. My only crystal-clear memory of the day was how intoxicatingly amazing Old Trafford was. And how amazing letting that piss out felt. It was an early lesson. Match day is all well and good, but you're never ever far from disaster. If your team doesn't let you down, you can bet something else will. So, take note of what I'm about to tell you, or prepare to sit next to me at the head table of the prat club.

## SKY WILL ALWAYS FUCK YOU

It was just a wedding. Alright, it was my brother's wedding, but this was the Manchester derby! The. Manchester. Derby. Even when I broke it down like that, my family still wasn't budging. 'Ooooooh, Mark, you can't miss your brother's wedding for a football match.' Piss off. But this put me in a very awkward position. Deep down, I blamed myself. I just hadn't done my homework.

I'd already learned the hard way to check the frickin' fixture list before confirming my attendance at any social events. Now I had mayonnaise all over my Chevy Chase. Back in 2001, U2 were playing a gig at Slane Castle in Ireland. My girlfriend at the time was a big fan, and so was I. (Don't start! They've got some bangers, alright! 'Where the Streets Have No Name', 'The Fly', 'Elevation'. Educate yourselves.) Anyway, I didn't need much persuading when she suggested we go. I was living in Dublin, and this was U-bloody-2 at Slane Castle! Fabrique Belgique, as Del Boy would say. Nevertheless, I wasn't stupid. I still checked the United fixture list in case there was a clash. Result! They didn't have a game that day! It was meant to be. We were all set. VIVA U2. But I had done something stupid. Really really fucking stupid.

United weren't playing that weekend. I'd got that one right. But England were playing Germany in Munich, the exact time U2 was taking the stage. This was September 2001. The days of Sven, Beckham, Owen, Gerrard . . . Chris Powell. Yeah, alright, I bloody know! VAR Check Complete. Decision: Total Prat. You know what happened next. You're not the Beast on *The Chase*, for fuck's sake.

I kidded myself that I could record the game and watch it afterwards without knowing the result. This was back in the days when that was realistic. No busybodies on social media or WhatsApp to tell you the score or what was going on. Unless someone texted you, you couldn't even look it up on your phone. Back then, we weren't glued to our phones either. They were so basic the only thing they doubled up as was a weapon.

I would also be in a crowd of Irish people who didn't care about England playing Germany. Most would rather drink bleach than watch that game. With all this in mind, as they would say in Dublin, I was fookin' grand. I could leave my phone at home, enjoy the gig, then watch the game afterwards, none the wiser. Boom! Boom! Boom! Let me hear you say wayo!

On the night, everything seemed to be going to plan. The gig was class, and no one had so much as mentioned the game. But when we were 10 metres away from our car, I heard some knobhead shout to their mate, 'Jesus . . . England beat Germany 5–1!' Thanks a fucking lot, pal. I was gutted. Not only did I know the result, but I had missed one of the great England games. How often do England go to Germany and hand their arses to them? After Italia 90 and Euro 96, I was desperate to get one over on them. And I'd missed it. Sure, I watched the game when I got back, but it wasn't the same. Watching a game when you already know the result is a bit like masturbating after having sex. Joyless.

As you might imagine, this had been a painful lesson. From that moment on, I always checked the fixture lists for United, England or even games in Siberia before committing to anything. For 15 years, my diligence had put me in good stead. Kid getting christened? Sorry, United are playing. Need me to work overtime? Sorry, England are playing. It's your uncle's funeral? Sorry, Vladivostok is playing.

So, when my brother told me he was getting married on a Saturday, I feared the worst. But when I checked the fixture list for any clash, I saw that United didn't have a game that day. Instead, they were playing the Manchester derby on the Sunday. Magnifique! The football gods were shining upon me. 'You're getting married. Lovely stuff. Of course, I'll be there.' I felt safe. Secure. No need to keep glancing at my phone for the score during the ceremony. People looking at me as if I'd shit the bed. No. I'd sit in the pews, maybe even shed a tear or two at true love, safe in the knowledge that I wasn't missing a thing. Then I could have a few drinks, dance to 'Agadoo' on the dance floor, tell a random stranger I loved them, eat my body weight in sausage rolls and still be fighting fit the next day for the Manchester derby. Carlsberg doesn't do perfect weekends, but this was very fucking close.

In recent years the derby game had also taken on a lot of significance. Before Sheikh Mansour decided to play Brewster's Millions with our insignificant neighbours, the derby was a bit of fun for United. It was like having a WWE fight with your skinny mate. Sure, he'd put up a good fight. It meant everything to him, but if he got a bit carried away, you'd put him in a Rowdy Roddy Piper sleeper hold and choke the fucker out. Show him just who was boss. The only time you'd lose was when you were a bit distracted. Like if you'd nailed a Big Mac meal and a strawberry milkshake just before doing battle, or if you couldn't be fucked and took pity on the poor guy giving it his all, puffing and panting, almost crying with frustration while you held him back with a finger to his forehead. That's how I used to see derby games anyway. I'd laugh at poor old Jeff Whitley while Giggs and Scholes ran rings around him. It was all just a bit of fun. The serious games were with the likes of Liverpool and Arsenal, maybe Chelsea from time to time. More often than not, you'd ruffle City's hair with a big grin on your face, wink and say, 'Good game,' as they trudged off the pitch to boos and humiliation. Alright, alright, I know City won a few derbies before the takeover, but United fans weren't that bothered. We were too busy winning titles to worry about Steve Lomas having the best night of his life.

However, by 2016, things had changed. Thanks to a bucket-load of money (which led to the club receiving a slap on the wrist from UEFA's financial fair play bean counters), City was packed with world-class players. In 2011 they even beat us 6–1 at Old Trafford on their way to winning the title. This was no longer just a derby game. City was our rival, and games against them would define our season.

As a United fan I was desperate to watch the game, but I also had another reason I couldn't miss it. In 2014 I had started doing *The United Stand* on YouTube. At the time, it was still just a side hustle while I juggled working a full-time job with the police. By 2016 I was probably still only attracting an audience of a few thousand per game, but it was growing every week. That season I had earmarked the derby game to really make a big splash and push my channel forward. So, with my brother's wedding on the Saturday, and the derby on the Sunday, I was all set for a weekend to remember. But then it all went wrong. Massimo Taibi wrong. It was as if the football gods poked their heads through the clouds, pointed their long fingers at me and said, 'See that smug little prick. Let's fuck his life up for a laugh.'

In their infinite wisdom, Sky decided that a Manchester derby on a Sunday afternoon didn't suit them. Instead, they'd rearrange it, for 12.30pm on the Saturday. You can imagine the scene in the boardroom at Sky HQ: 'Carragher has a Sunday roast planned so let's move the game to the Saturday.' Anyway, whatever the reasons, they certainly didn't take into account poor Mark Goldbridge, who had already dug his own grave and had confirmed he would be more than happy to attend his brother's wedding at the exact time as the Manchester derby.

The injustice hit me like Didier Drogba with a Danish referee. I couldn't miss the derby or the chance to boost my fledgling channel. This was important stuff. Massive football match mixed with major work opportunity. Then, I breathed a sigh of relief. I realised that while the derby kicked off at

12.30, the wedding ceremony didn't begin until 1.30. This might just work. I could watch the whole game, miss the church bit of the wedding, then arrive in time for the reception festivities, with no one any the wiser. It wasn't like I was the best man or anything. There was no pressing need for me to be at the church, handing over rings, winking at the bridesmaids. Like Marouane Fellaini, I wouldn't be missed. I breathed a sigh of relief. It was going to be OK. My brother was a good man. Surely, he would understand.

Did he fuck.

I was working in London when I decided to call and casually give him the news.

'Yeah, y'know, the wedding. I'll miss the church bit, but I'll see you at the reception afterwards.'

'Why?'

'United are playing at 12.30.'

'So?'

'It's the Manchester derby.'

'And?'

I looked at my phone, thinking the reception must be off.

'It's the Manchester derby,' I repeated.

'I heard you.'

'Well, it'll be over by two, so I'll be at the reception.'

'I want you at the church.'

In a street full of people, I stopped dead. Was he having a laugh? Completely oblivious to my surroundings, I raised my voice slightly. When the going gets tough, Goldbridge gets rough.

'Why do you need me at the church?'

'It's important.'

'I'm not even an usher or anything. I won't be missed.'

'You're my brother.'

I didn't handle the next bit so well.

'You're telling me that when you're at the altar, getting married to the love of your life, you'll be looking over at me, picking my nose in the third row.'

Silence. I'd made my point. Now, to soften him up a bit. This was man management from the school of Sir Alex Ferguson. Twat them hard, then put a hand on the shoulder.

'I'll be there for the reception,' I said. 'We'll have a right good drink. We'll be doing "The Final Countdown" on the dancefloor by six.'

'I need you at the church, Mark.'

'For fuck's sake!'

I totally lost my head after this. I was like Richard Ashcroft in the video for 'Bitter Sweet Symphony'. I was so caught up in the moment that I was bumping into people, walls, crossing the street without looking. My head was gone, like Gazza in a hotel room after missing out on France 98. But there was no two ways about it. My brother wanted me at the church. It wasn't just my brother either. Within minutes of hanging up, I had my mum on the phone.

'What's all this about you not coming to the wedding?'

'I'm going to the reception, but I need to miss the church so I can livestream my reaction to the Manchester derby for my YouTube channel.'

'What do you mean?'

Here was another life lesson. Don't ever try to explain YouTube to people who have never watched it before. It's the equivalent of Pep Guardiola trying to coach Gabby Agbonlahor. They might smile and nod, but they just don't get it.

'It's your brother's wedding, Mark.'

So that was that. Swivel on that, Mark, you big prick. Yet, while I was down, I certainly wasn't out. I had a cunning plan. I realised that I could still watch the first half before I had to get to the church. Although I soon wished I hadn't bothered.

With just 36 minutes of the game gone, I was actually looking forward to the wedding. United were two goals down and playing like they'd lose a game of hide and seek to Stevie Wonder. It was like Jedis against Jar Jar Binks. 'Weeza shit.' Spain has El Clásico, well, this was El Crapico. But, just as I was giving up hope, Ibrahimović pulled a goal back on the stroke of half-time. The second half was all set to be a belter, and muggins here was going to miss it.

As the second half kicked off, and with United in the ascendancy, I couldn't hold it off any longer. Right in the middle of a watch-along, I cut the feed. 'Oh no! Bloody

Virgin! Buggering me up again.' I'm telling you, I gave Ken Barlow a run for his money with acting like that.

I set off for the church like Dan James. 'Meep fucking Meep.' Roadrunner's on his way. And you guessed it. While I was sitting there, a sweating, breathless mess of a man, missing the second half, the bride got stuck in traffic and didn't turn up until 3pm! United lost 2–1 as well. Of course they bloody did. Sod being at a wedding. I felt like I was at a funeral. Fucking bury me.

In all fairness, the wedding was actually good fun in the end. It certainly helped me get over my misery, but this was still a crucial lesson for any football fan. Always check the fixture list before committing to anything, and even then, just remember, Sky will always try and fuck you.

## AN ODE TO BRYAN GUNN

Let's take a moment to recap what we've learned so far. You've checked the fixture list so you can watch the match. Congratulations. You've ticked a major no-prat box. You've also got some decent players in, and your team has had a blinding pre-season, so you're bang up for the new season. As Hot Chocolate would say, 'Everyone's a winner, baby, and that's the truth.' You couldn't be more excited. Wipe that smug smile off your face, you massive twat. What the fuck are you doing? Seriously. Sit the fuck down. You're heading for disaster, and you don't even know it.

Like I said before, pre-season has its own magic, but it's sort of like the freak show before the real thing begins. It's been three long months and counting since you last saw a league game. In the meantime, you've bought the new shirt, had the new signing's name and number printed on the back, picked a Fantasy Team and you're feeling so positive you even put a tenner on your team to win the title. Then, you take your seat in the glorious sunshine . . . and the horror unfolds. Rather than playing like vintage Brazil, it looks like someone has fed laxatives to cows and let them loose on the pitch. Shit everywhere. It really doesn't get any worse than Norwich City in 2009.

After being relegated from the Championship at the end of the 2008/9 season, the Canaries appointed club legend Bryan Gunn as manager. Pre-season results had been decent and, with a few new signings, it was thought Norwich would be pushing for the League One title. For a big club like Norwich to be in League One was seen as a temporary inconvenience. They were expecting to swat teams aside, especially in the first fixture when they faced local rivals Colchester United at Carrow Road. It was like The Rock taking on Olly Murs in a no-holds-barred cage match. You don't know how much I'd pay to see that, by the way.

For most of the club's history, Colchester has been scrambling around the bottom tiers of English football, like shit at the bottom of the birdcage. They had no great hopes of promotion and probably would have taken a plucky defeat at Norwich. But what happened next was one of the great all-time football clusterfucks. Norwich slumped to a 7–1 defeat at home to their lowly rivals in the first game of the season. It was like taking a dump in your own hands and clapping. I mean, what the fucking hell are you supposed to do with that?

I tell you what you do, you sack the bloody manager! And that's just what Norwich did. Gunn was shown the door . . . and replaced by Colchester manager Paul Lambert! You know what they say: if you can't beat them, join them – or rob them blind. Either way, it worked like a charm. Despite this horrific start to the season, Norwich still won the title with 95 points!

This also goes to show that whatever the result, the opening day of the season is never a great indicator of how your team is going to fare. Plenty of teams that have shit the bed on the opening day have gone on to have successful seasons. It's essential to keep some perspective and not immediately jump onto social media and have a rant. I hold my hands up here. I've been there. I've done it. I still do! There are just far too many emotions swimming around on opening day. You can lose all perspective. New signings aren't given a chance to find their feet. Managers are out of their depth. Even your fellow fans can be in the firing line, turning on each other like Lee

Bowyer and Kieron Dyer. The disappointment and betrayal take a while to work through the system.

But take a look at United in 1995. After a summer of selling off key players like Mark Hughes, Andrei Kanchelskis and Paul Ince, Sir Alex didn't bring anyone in to replace them. Our first game was Villa away, and our young team crashed to a 3–1 defeat. It was a total disaster. Breadsticks against light-sabers. Questions about Sir Alex were even being asked. The season before, we had finished runners-up in the league and the Cup. At best, we now looked like a team in transition. Some even felt that the brief golden period was over. On *Match of the Day* that night, Alan Hansen famously quipped, 'You don't win anything with kids.'

Well, Alan, you bloody do when those kids are Paul Scholes, Ryan Giggs, David Beckham, Nicky Butt, and Gary and Phil Neville. After that disastrous opening day defeat, United went on to win the double. 'Glory Glory Man United . . . Glory Glory Man United . . .'

## FERGIE TIME

Imagine you were watching the film *Seven* in the cinema and, with five minutes left, thought, *Well, Pitt and Freeman have caught Kevin Spacey now. The movie's over. I might as well leave to beat the traffic.* You big prat. [SPOILER ALERT] You've missed Gwyneth Paltrow's head in a box. In. a. box! What are you leaving early for anyway? To cut the bloody grass? Is it really worth it?

Now, I'm not saying every movie will end like *Seven*. I mean, come on! Some might end like the last bloody Bond movie, but the point remains. You just never know what shit is going to go down. And in football, things are even more unpredictable than anything Hollywood can come up with. Not even the best scriptwriters in the world could have conjured up 'Fergie Time'.

The phenomenon of 'Fergie Time' was officially born on 10 April 1993. At that point in the season, we were neck and neck with Villa in a chase for the title – and, of course, we can't do things fucking easy. United were playing Sheffield Wednesday at Old Trafford, and the score was tied after 90 minutes. Dropping points at this late stage of the season would put us in the mud. With seven minutes of injury time added on and Fergie frantically urging everyone forward, staring oblivion in the face, Steve Bruce powered home a header. Mayhem ensued. Fergie did a little jig on the touchline while Brian Kidd sunk to his knees and raised his fists towards the heavens. Absolute filth. It belongs on the top shelf. With this, United was back on track for its first top-flight title in 26 years. But Fergie Time was just getting started.

The following year, United repeated the trick in the FA Cup semi-final at Wembley against Oldham Athletic. With the score at 0–1 to Oldham, and with just one minute of extra time remaining, Mark Hughes stretched out a leg and fired home a sensational volley to save United from defeat. Three days later, United beat Oldham 4–1 in the replay, on their way to winning the Cup.

'Fergie Time' was now officially a thing. You just couldn't stop it. With the game all but over, Fergie's boys would somehow clutch victory from the jaws of defeat. Time and time again, this happened. There are many examples, but these are some of my favourites.

In 1999 United looked to be heading out of the Cup in the fourth round when we found ourselves 1–0 down to Liverpool with just minutes to go. Dwight Yorke equalised in the 88th minute, then super-sub himself Ole Gunnar Solskjaer grabbed the winner.

A 'Fergie Time' winner against Liverpool is always one to savour, as is one in the Manchester derby, and none have been sweeter than Michael Owen's 96th-minute winner in a 4–3 win over City in 2009. Sit down, ya twats. Put some glue on your seat, Sellotape on your pants, and sit bloody down!

Then, in April 2009, United found itself in a three-way title chase with Liverpool and Chelsea. Before our home game against Villa, Liverpool had won and gone top of the league. God, they were un-bloody-bearable that season. If you remember, this was the year Rafa got his bloody knickers in a twist and went on his 'facts' rant about Fergie. Like

Kevin Keegan before him, Fergie had him hook, line and sinker. Anyway, we needed to win, but with just seconds to spare, the score was tied. Never afraid to roll the dice, Fergie sent on 17-year-old Federico Macheda for his first team debut. He didn't disappoint. Receiving the ball from Giggs on the edge of the box, he turned his marker brilliantly before curling the ball into the far corner of the goal. Pour a pint over my bloody head and give me that big fat tasty title!

Yet, of course, the mother of all Fergie Time goals came in the 1999 Champions League final. Losing 1–0 to Bayern Munich, United looked dead and buried, with just three minutes of injury time to play. Against the run of play, Teddy Sheringham improbably equalised in the 90th minute before Ole Gunnar Solskjaer poked home the winner a minute later. 'You only sing when you're winning. Sing when you're wiiiiiiinnnniinnnnggg!'

'Fergie Time' is now a part of football folklore. You'd never ever leave a game early when Fergie was in charge. During his glorious reign, United scored 81 goals in the Premier League in injury time, including 16 winners. But despite United's reputation for last-gasp heroics, plenty of others have got in on the act as well. Arsenal actually scored 19 winners in injury time during this time, while Liverpool scored 24. Other teams have scored iconic last-minute goals as well, including Manchester City . . .

I can't face talking about 'that' one right now, so let's focus on the 1999 Second Division play-off final against Gillingham instead. As the game ticked into the 90th minute, Gillingham were two goals up and heading to the Championship. Kevin Horlock then pulled a goal back before Paul Dickov, in the fifth minute of injury time, equalised with the last kick of the game. By that stage, City fan Noel Gallagher had already given up and was heading away from Wembley in a taxi. When he heard Dickov had equalised he rushed back and arrived just in time to see City win on penalties. Plenty of other fans weren't so lucky. They probably didn't even know City had won until they got home later that night. Don't look back in anger . . .

There have been countless other iconic last-minute winners over the years, just as dramatic as United and City. In 1999 goalkeeper Jimmy Glass scored the winner for Carlisle to keep them in the Football League. In the 2013 Championship play-off semi-finals, Troy Deeney scored the winner with the last kick of the game, just seconds after Leicester had missed a penalty. And who can forget David Beckham's free kick against Greece to send England to the 2002 World Cup? Or Michael Thomas's last-gasp goal at Anfield in 1989 to win the title for Arsenal. Even Spurs have got in on the act, with Lucas Moura's last-second goal against Ajax taking them to the Champions League final in 2019.

All this goes to prove that you should never ever leave a game early, even in the most dire circumstances. I can't really blame Spurs fans for leaving St James' Park in April 2023 when their team was 5–0 down after 20 minutes. It's a long way back to London on a Sunday evening. You might as well hit the road and save yourself from watching Eric Dier stumble around like a man trying to eat his feet for the remaining 70 minutes. I understand why you might leave early in such situations, but has football taught you nothing!?

Take Newcastle vs Arsenal in 2011, for instance. At half-time, Newcastle were 4–0 down against an Arsenal team going for the title. It seemed a lost cause, but in the greatest Premier League comeback of all time, the game finished 4–4. Then, there was Manchester City against Spurs in the fourth round of the Cup in 2004. At half-time, City were not only three goals down but also had Joey Barton sent off during the interval for dissent. Quelle surprise. So, away from home, losing 3–0 and down to ten men, you can bet quite a number of City fans left. Absolute cretins. Somehow, and against all odds, City won the game 4–3, in what might be the most Spursy result of all time. They just can't help themselves, can they? One of my favourite comebacks also saw United 3–0 down to Spurs at White Hart Lane at half-time before scoring five goals without reply in the second half. There's a pattern emerging here, Spurs fans . . .

Let all this serve as an invaluable lesson to you. If you want to see the equivalent of Gwyneth Paltrow's head in a box, never ever leave a game early.

## WATCHING PARTNERS

We've all been there, in the stadium, at the pub or even in the sanctuary of our own home. You're trying to watch the game, and some absolute dickhead next to you is doing your head in. It can't be helped. You didn't choose to have them blathering in your ear for two hours. If there's someone talking nonsense on social media, you can ignore or block them. It's one of the great tragedies that we don't possess a real-life block button. Someone opens their piehole, and you just hold up your block button, leaving them to nod in recognition and disappear back into the shadows, like Alan Pardew at a job interview. Sadly, in such situations, you're left with three options:

1. Grin and bear it like you're watching the latest Marvel film;
2. Try to engage with the individual in an attempt to get them to see sense; or,
3. Fart and hope they move. Just be careful not to follow through.

But you can avoid these stages altogether if you know what to look for. Granted, you can't avoid some knobhead randomly sitting next to you during the match, but you can vet any friends or family who might want to join you. You've just got to know the various football personalities and understand how compatible you are with each one. A word of warning, though. This might make some of you uncomfortable, as it's pretty much a knobhead test. If you're in two categories or above, then guess what; you're the knobhead.

## SOFA ULTRAS

These prats turn up in the latest kit, pro edition, maybe even a scarf, and they just don't shut the fuck up. They're the type to try and start a Mexican wave in the fucking living room. If they're not ramming facts and trivia down your throat, then they're setting traps, asking you ridiculous questions to show you up in your own bloody home.

'Which player took the first throw-in in Manchester United's history?'

'I'm trying to watch the game.'

'Seriously, you don't know this?'

Before you know it, you're smothering the smug little fucker with a pillow. You're Arsenal till you die? Well, fucking die then! At last, you can watch the game in peace. You'll deal with the consequences later.

## MINI NEVILLE

One Gary Neville is more than enough, thank you. You don't need another opinionated statto chatting shit in your ear. You know what you're dealing with as soon as they show up. This lot usually dresses like they're ready for a night on the gantry. No replica shirt. They're like a reject model from the Next catalogue.

They tend not to get too carried away with the game. They're almost detached. Like they're above it. As if you're their audience and they're gracing you with their knowledge. These prats are also total fucking anoraks who seem to be able to back everything up with stats. It's enough to make you neck a bottle of Imodium Plus and sit on the bog for the rest of the game, wallowing in the smell of your own shit. They might come up with an interesting point or two, but the next day you'll be reading something from the *Athletic* or *Mundial* and realise they've ripped it off. Cheeky fuckers. Don't think I don't see you.

## GRUMPASAURUS

'What are you fucking doing?' 'I told you we should have sold him.' 'He's fucking shit!'

Nothing is good enough for these prats. If Father Christmas gave them a Mega Drive and a Super NES for Christmas, they'd still cry for a Neo Geo. Even when their team is winning they get no joy from it. That's because winning isn't the aim of the game for this lot. They actually *want* their team to lose. They want to feel superior, and they need a reason to unload. Football is the only chance in their lives when they get to vent and go full Neil Warnock, right in your fucking ear hole. Just settle the fuck down and enjoy the game, alright. And stop chatting to the dog while you're at it. It's getting awkward.

## FANTO FANATIC

We all have a Fantasy Football team, but some of us can still enjoy the game. Not these bunch of pricks. Fantasy Football has taken over their lives. The game isn't about the result anymore. It's all about their players getting points. Every single bloody thing is viewed through this prism. Worse still, they're probably in a WhatsApp group with you as well, so you don't only have to listen to their shite in real life, but they'll also repeat it in the group.

'I knew I should have captained Salah. The thing is, I checked his stats against . . .'

BLAH, BLAH, BLAH. You're not Pep, pal. You're John from the bank who hates his wife and drives a Fiat. In real life, you'd be tactically masterminded by Steve bloody Bruce. Now, put your phone down and watch the bloody game.

## EVERY-TWO-YEARS FAN

This lot emerges every two years like a drunk badger from hibernation. 'Oh, is it that time to act like a knobhead again? I better get my England shirt out.'

Usually, these 'fans' don't give a toss about football. But as soon as the Euros or the World Cup roll up, there they fucking are, like a Michael Bublé Christmas album. They're bloody sneaky, this lot. They know they'll be social outcasts for the next month if they don't jump on the bandwagon. That's all well and good, but they can't just watch the game and admit they know nothing. They go and buy a new England shirt and start chatting absolute shit.

'Does Harry Kane still play for Manchester United?'

'No, Mum! For fuck's sake. I'm trying to watch the game.'

While you might humour them for a bit, it's the crocodile tears that get me. You can guarantee England will somehow fuck it up, and this prick will have tears rolling down his cheeks. Fucking hell! I'm the one who's done the hard yards here. I've seen Michael Ricketts play for England! I've earned this pain. Get back in your box.

## THE BUBBLE BURSTERS

These pricks not only don't like football, but are determined to burst your bubble as well. They say silly fucking things like: 'I don't see the point. Twenty-two people chasing a ball around the pitch.' Listen up, alright! This is all I have! Don't make me realise my life's passion is bloody ridiculous. This is the pact all football fans have made. It's a charade. No one must ever pierce the illusion that this isn't all vitally important stuff. Professor fucking Snape turning up in my living room isn't going to make me realise it's a silly game.

'Oh yeah, now that you mention it, football's a load of bollocks, isn't it. Shall we fuck off the Manchester derby and watch *Love Island* instead?'

Seriously . . .

## BEING BLOCKED BY GARY LINEKER

Speaking of people being annoying . . .

No matter how good a game might be, a pundit can make or break it. Some can enhance the viewing experience (like yours truly); others can have you smashing up your living room. If you're going to enjoy watching a game without kicking the TV in, then you need to know your pundits: those you enjoy, those you can endure and those who make your eyes bleed. Let's take a quick look at the evolution of the pundit so we know just what we're dealing with here and why it's got so bad.

Pundits first became a thing during the 1970 World Cup. There'd never been anything like it before. Previously, a standard televised match had a commentator and a presenter, and that was pretty much that, as basic as you like. It was The White Stripes compared to Queen. But ITV's 1970 World Cup panel of Malcolm Allison, Derek Dougan, Pat Crerand and Bob McNab caused a sensation. All were colourful, knowledgeable characters who weren't afraid to speak their minds. Looking back now, that tournament's games are extraordinary to listen to. These guys had no media training whatsoever. They'd have a few drinks before coming on air and then let rip. It didn't matter who they upset. And no one told them to tone it down. It was electric.

The star of the show was Allison, who made it very clear he wasn't a fan of England's Alan Mullery. Every opportunity he got, he savaged him. Mullery was so fucked off with this he came on the show for a showdown! Chomping on a cigar, Allison still didn't back down as he forensically demolished Mullery's game to his face. This was absolute box office. Imagine a pundit or a player doing this today. How much would we have loved Paul Pogba to have a sit-down with Graeme Souness? Viewers lapped it up because it was like watching real fans talk. The former players weren't sanitised or trained to say certain things. As pundits, they could just go off on one without worrying about the consequences, no matter who their rants might offend.

We could not be further away from this now. Instead of being upfront, pundits trot out safe clichés and do everything possible to avoid upsetting anyone. Worse still, even though they're ex-professionals, they don't even seem to have a bloody clue what they're talking about half the time.

There are multiple offenders when it comes to modern pundits who make me want to smother myself in ketchup and jump into a shark tank. Michael Owen and Jermaine Jenas are probably the worst. Listening to them is like inflicting poison in my ears. Owen is a bad pundit at the best of times. I don't even know what he's doing on TV. For the last few years of his career, he didn't even seem interested in football. But if you are going to be on TV, at least be good at your job instead of just being there because you used to be a decent player a few years ago. Go and look after your horses, Michael. Put yourself out of your misery.

However, while Owen is out of his depth, Jermaine Jenas is the one who really gets on my tits. When United fans protested against the Glazers trying to join the Super League in 2021 and succeeded in getting the home game against Liverpool postponed, most right-thinking fans thought this was a just cause. Not Jermaine 'Power to the People' Jenas. He not only slammed the fans by saying they'd 'overstepped the mark' but then added insult to injury and defended the Glazers because 'they'd spent a lot of money'. Congratulations, Jermaine. You've done it. You've let angry Mark out of his cage, and now we have to get into the Glazers.

When the Glazers purchased Manchester United in 2005,

they hardly used any of their own money. The club bought itself. It's insane but true. Worse still, it's entirely legal. In a highly leveraged takeover, the Glazers took out bank loans to buy the club. Once they had done so, they let the club pick up the tab. United was debt-free before the takeover, but after this, the club was loaded with more than £500 million in debt and had to pay an enormous amount of interest on top. It has reportedly since cost the club over £750 million and counting to service that debt, which the Glazers ran up just to buy the club. And United have had no benefit from this whatsoever.

Adding insult to injury, while the Glazers have paid themselves, according to some estimates, £50 million in directors' fees, since 2016, they've also paid out more than £150 million in dividends from the club, mostly to themselves. They are, according to the *Athletic*, the only owners in the Premier League to regularly pay out significant dividends rather than reinvest the money into the club. Even during the COVID-19 pandemic, with fans locked out of stadiums and the club making a loss of £23 million, the *Guardian* reported, these shameless chancers still made sure they got paid millions of pounds, plunging the club further into debt.

Meanwhile, as every major European club upgrades their stadiums, Old Trafford is a rotting mess. The state of it is seriously embarrassing. That's before we even get to our training ground at Carrington. Cristiano Ronaldo left the club in 2009, but when he returned in 2021, he said nothing had changed. In fact, it had gone backwards. The gym facilities were so bad that he even joined a local gym to have access to the best equipment. Just compare United's facilities to what Spurs offer their players. Their stadium is up there with the best in the world, while their training facilities are like that of a five-star hotel. Spurs last won a major trophy in 2008 and haven't won the league since 1961, so what's United's excuse?

Now for those of you feverishly raising your hand, screaming out, 'Acshually, the Glazers have spent more money than any other club in the last decade,' let me stop you right there. You're making yourself look a right twat. Firstly, the Glazers aren't spending their own money. It's money the club has generated itself. Between 2012 and 2021, United's owners put in less money than any other owner in the Premier League. While Man City received a £684 million cash injection and Chelsea £516 million, United's owners took £154 million out!

Secondly, *yes*, we might have spent money, but the transfer policy is a total disaster. It's all short-termism. There's no grand plan. Look at how, over the last five years, Real Madrid has been stockpiling the best midfield talent in the world. Thanks to this, they now boast the likes of Valverde, Tchouaméni, Bellingham and Camavinga. United helped Madrid fund this by taking the likes of an injury-prone Varane off their hands and offering a 31-year-old Casemiro a five-year contract, at the bargain price of £60 million. I mean, for fuck's sake. Madrid saw us fucking coming, didn't they? Lube yourself up, lads. The Madrid gang is in town, and they're really horny.

All the Glazers look at is the present. Put enough sticky tape over the team so it's in contention for the top four, and that'll do. They only spend when things look to be going down the pan. Lose to Brighton and Brentford, then push the panic button and spend £86 million on Antony. Just throw a pint of sick in my face. It's the same old shit all the time. This frantic spending meant they had no cash for transfer fees in January 2023, so they could only sign Weghorst and Marcel Sabitzer . . . on loan. We might as well put on our clown pants and join the bloody circus instead of trying to win a title.

Do you see any other major club regularly loaning players like Odion Ighalo, Wout Weghorst, Sergio Reguilón and Sofyan Amrabat? It's no wonder that with a transfer policy like this, we've finished outside the top four in five of the last ten seasons since Sir Alex retired. In contrast, before the Glazers arrived, the lowest United had finished in the Premier League was third.

So, there you have it. In black and fucking white. Stick that in your pipe and smoke it, Jermaine Jenas. And yet, despite all of this information, which is very easy to find, Jenas thought it just to have a pop at the protesting fans for 'overstepping the mark', all while our taxes provided him with a platform to do so. Do me a favour.

Sorry, where were we? What year is it? See what you've made me do, Jermaine. I've totally lost my thread now. Ah, yes, pundits. Fucking hell, this is only going to get worse, isn't it . . .

You might think that out of all the pundits out there, I would hate Graeme Souness and Jamie Carragher the most. *Oooooh, look at me. I played for Liverpool, and I hate United.* Christ, they talk a load of bollocks sometimes. We all remember Souness's campaign against Paul Pogba. All Pogba had to do was breathe and Souness was blaming him for global warming. Throw in a crazy new hairstyle every week and a bucket-load of horror show performances and Souness was ready to explode at the mere mention of his name. The thing is, I respect it. Just as I respect Carragher giving shit to Gary Neville non-stop as well. Now, I'm not saying I like it. I'd go to war against the two of them, but I'd take it over the bland, sanitised, uninformed pundit any day. Souness and Carragher merely represent what most of us football fans are like. We're all biased towards our team and enjoy a bit of shithousery against our rivals. At the very least, it makes for good television.

Conversely, it might shock you to learn that I have an issue with some of the pundits with a link to United. Now, some of them are decent at being pundits. Neville and Keane are particularly good in this regard. Neville clearly does his homework, while Keane is prepared to call it as he sees it. Both can make for cracking television. But the thing that really disappointed me was the refusal of nearly all United pundits, including Neville and Keane, to criticise Ole Gunnar Solskjaer when he was United manager. I get it. He's their mate, and they don't want to stick the sword in when he's having a bad time. He's also a United legend, and we all love Ole, don't we? When he was sacked, it felt like killing Bambi. But while they all held off having a pop at Ole, that didn't stop them going for Moyes, Van Gaal, Mourinho, Ten Hag or any other manager in the league. Towards the end of Solskjaer's tenure, it got ridiculous. Ole could have farted in Neville's face and he would have found a way to compliment the smell. Again, what is the point of being a well-paid pundit if you're not going to give an honest and informed opinion?

The pundits that particularly wind me up, though, are those that offer nothing. No tactical analysis, no personality, no willingness to rock the boat. Does anyone even know Alan Smith exists? I think even Sky has forgotten he's there, although maybe it's all just a big wind-up. Some bloke at Sky is clearly wondering how long subscribers will continue to pay hundreds of pounds a year for football while making them fall asleep to the monotone voice of Alan Smith. At least show some enthusiasm, Alan. There's more excitement at a James Milner house party.

But, of all the pundits out there, my congratulations go to ex-referee Dermot Gallagher. You win Goldbridge's grand prize for being totally fucking pointless. Poor Dermot can usually be found looking bewildered on Sky Sports News on

Monday mornings, analysing the weekend's refereeing decisions. I don't know why people bother to watch. Even if a referee had committed a gangland hit live on television, Gallagher would still say, 'At the end of the day, you've got to say it was a justified action and within the spirit of the game.'

On the one hand, I respect his loyalty to his colleagues. Being a referee is a hard job, and they take far too much abuse. But this makes for crap television. Gallagher is there to use his experience and knowledge to analyse a situation and provide an impartial view. If he's just going to stand up for referees and attempt to justify their decisions, particularly when VAR has had multiple views (we'll get to VAR later) and still fucked it up, then what's the point of him being there? He's like a red traffic light on *Grand Theft Auto*. Useless!

Now, I'm not just here to slag off every pundit and then say, 'Look at me! I'm great.' Well, I mean, I am, and I am, but I'm not a total prick. There are still some great pundits around. Ally McCoist is the shining example. No matter the game, he's always buzzing with excitement. There's a sense of fun when he commentates. He loves a joke but is as enthralled by a player doing something special as the average fan. You genuinely feel that even if he wasn't being paid to work at the game, he might have just turned up to watch anyway.

Now wait a fucking minute, I hear some of you cry, what about our saint and lord Gary Lineker? Well, hold your horses. England's big shining light doesn't get away that easily.

Lineker is probably the most famous pundit in the country. As the anchor – yes, I said anchor – of *Match of the Day*, as well as the BBC's football coverage in general, he certainly gets well-paid by the taxpayer. And I find it hard to knock Gary. When I was a kid, he was one of my heroes, banging in goals for England, and he's made the transition to television look seamless. I'm sure there are plenty of kids who watch him today who have no idea he used to play. To them, he's a professional football presenter and always has been. As far as that goes, he's pretty decent as well. Listen, there's far worse out there. Sadly, he's not one for debate.

When Casemiro scandalously got sent off against Crystal Palace in February 2023, I calmly and sensibly laid out my reasons on Twitter for it being harsh. Alright, I went full Goldbridge, but it was justified, and it was on my own Twitter page, so I can say what I like. But St Gary, our arbiter of truth, thought differently, and from that moment on, it appears I was blocked. Maybe it was this tweet, or perhaps it's because I made a joke about him pooing his pants against Ireland in the World Cup. It's true. Look it up on YouTube if you have the stomach for it. Either way, he blocked me. C'mon now, Gary, let's kiss and make up.

However, Gary Lineker isn't alone. There are plenty of other pundits, or people in the media, who seem to have a problem with a fan expressing their views. Even while I've been happily writing this book, I have suddenly come under attack. Former United and England star Paul Parker has been very vocal about his feelings about me and my content. Danny Murphy has decided to stick his oar in as well. As the great Wealdstone Raider would say, 'Ya fuckin' want some? Do ya?' Well bring your fucking dinner.

I have no problem with anyone having an opinion about my content. You live and die by the sword, and football fans will always have very different opinions. It's part of what makes the game great. Sadly, these attacks feel more personal and tend to come from a place where an ex-professional feels that someone who hasn't played the game to the same level doesn't deserve to have an opinion. This is one of my pet hates. 'What does Mark Goldbridge, or any fan, know about football? He's not played at the level I have.'

Let's just break this shithousery down. Playing the game and analysing it are two very, very different things. Just the same as you don't need to be a cow to appreciate a good steak. You don't have to have played at the highest level to analyse the game well. All you need is a dedication to watching and learning as much as possible about it. Watch games at all levels. Read books. Watch tactical videos on YouTube. Most fans do far more of this than a footballer might do in their lifetime. Players are often geared up just to focus on themselves and prepare for how they're going to play. Some can't even be bothered to do that. At Chelsea, Eden Hazard often turned up on match day, not knowing who they would play. Plenty of footballers also admit they don't even like the game. Benoît Assou-Ekotto at Spurs and Ben White at Arsenal have openly said they don't watch football. Even those pundits who seem really clued up on the game often have their research done for them by an army of statisticians hired by a broadcaster.

Just because someone has played at a higher level than a fan, do you think that automatically means their opinions on football count more than a fan who is devoted to learning about the game? There are now countless managers who have never played the game at a professional level but are doing very well for themselves. Just look at 31-year-old Will Still, currently the head coach of Ligue 1 club Reims. Still has never played any level of professional football, but after becoming obsessed with *Championship Manager*, he devoted himself to becoming a manager. Initially working with Preston's U-14 team in England, he worked his way through various roles before being appointed as the manager of Reims in 2022. At the time, he still didn't have his UEFA Pro Licence. Much of what he was coaching was based on his own analysis and from playing *Championship Manager*. Despite this, he set a new Ligue 1 record, going his first 17 matches undefeated. Whose opinion are you taking? Danny Murphy, because he carried Steven Gerrard's boot bag over a decade ago, or Will Still, who has never played one minute of professional football? Thank you, and good night. Goldbridge has left the building.

Of course, fans can say silly things sometimes. Even I'm

not immune to it. My nonsense usually gets turned into a meme or a GIF to constantly beat me over the head with. No one is right all of the time. Not even the likes of Paul Parker and Danny Murphy. Even some of the greats have dropped some absolute clangers. Neil Warnock once said Sol Bamba was better than Virgil Van Dijk. Sir Alex Ferguson claimed Phil Jones would be the next Duncan Edwards. Pelé somehow came to the conclusion in 1995 that Nicky Barmby was going to be as good as Roberto Baggio. And then there is Garth Crooks . . .

Crooks was a decent player for Spurs in his day, following which he pivoted to work as a pundit for the BBC, where his picks for his 'Team of the Week' have continually bleached my eyes. Of course, he's entitled to his opinion, even if he's having a giraffe. One time, he picked Liverpool's Joel Matip, claiming that in the game against Spurs, 'He survived one or two scary moments but did enough against Spurs to help seal the win.' There was just one problem with this. Matip wasn't even in the bloody squad! He wasn't even in the stadium! I despair. I really do.

All of the above is why so many people have now gravitated towards fan entertainment, like *The United Stand*. They're sick and tired of the arrogance of the old boys' clubs and bland questions and answers that any of us could come up with. Fan channels aren't beholden to anyone. We can say it exactly as we see it, no matter who we might upset. We don't have Sky, the Premier League, the PFA or anyone else down our earholes trying to control us.

So, just remember, you don't have to watch the pundits if you don't want to. The mute button is always handy, especially when Jermaine Jenas is on. Fire up your phone or laptop instead, and put on a fan channel as they do a live watch-along. More often than not, it's far more informed and entertaining than what the mainstream broadcasters can offer. And you'll get to see me lose my shit on a regular basis while blaming my inadvertent trumps on my cat. Beat that, Gary Neville.

## PROPER FaNz

Alright, here we go. Repeat after me. 'You're still a real fan if you don't go to games.' This shouldn't be a hard concept to grasp, but for some, it's like teaching cats to bark.

Let me break this down for those who just can't get their pretty heads around it. Manchester United have 1.1 billion fans and followers worldwide. Old Trafford's capacity is 74,310. This means that only 0.006 per cent of the club's fans can fit into the stadium. And for most, attending games regularly just isn't realistic. Many fans live hundreds, if not thousands, of miles away. That's before we even get into the cost of going to a game these days. In short, you've got more chance of enjoying a wank from Edward Scissorhands than getting a match day ticket.

I love going to Old Trafford. There's nothing like going to a live game, soaking up the atmosphere and watching world-class footballers, and Scott McTominay, in the flesh. In the past, I'd always try to get to United games at least four to five times a season. Even then, cost and family commitments meant I couldn't go as much as I would have liked. These days, it's even more difficult for me to attend owing to my streams for *The United Stand* YouTube channel. Of course, I miss not being able to get to the stadium – even one where the roof is leaking – but there's no shame in watching games on television. You're still a real fan. And there are plenty of benefits. You can mark out your cosy corner on the sofa for a long, hard day watching your team, cup of tea in hand, and with easy access to the toilet. Bliss. That's as long as the bastard internet doesn't go down. This has killed me on more than one occasion, most memorably during France versus England in the 2022 World Cup quarter-final.

For the match, I was doing a live watch-along with more than 100,000 live viewers at the time that England won the second penalty. We were losing 2–1 and with just six minutes remaining, it was fucking crucial that we scored; otherwise, we were as good as out. I watched Harry Kane put the ball down on the spot, take three steps back, exhale and then . . .

'For fuck's sake!'

My bloody stream went down!

Bloody typical. A big moment like this and Virgin decided to fuck me. Isn't that ironic? This would be a disaster at the best of times, but when thousands of people are watching you react to a massively important penalty, it's a monumental calamity. At United Stand Towers, we went to DEFCON 1. This was an all-out emergency. Thankfully, I had my tech team ready to take care of such a situation with a state-of-the-art solution.

'Fucking work, you twat!'

Swearing repeatedly at the monitor, I slapped the screen, shook the router and frantically turned it off and on again. Of course, when I turned off the router, the game went down as well. What are you doing, you prat? Seriously?

Putting the router back on, the game suddenly came back, and so was I. I just hoped I wasn't a meme already. Some prick had probably taken the freeze-frame of my face and conjured up some fucking witty comment, already spiralling around cyberspace at my expense.

Thankfully, I was OK on the meme front, but the score still said France 2 England 1. 'You what?' Then it dawned on me. Kane must have missed. *You fucking dickhead!* I was fuming. Not only at the miss and looking like an idiot in the middle of a livestream, but also at missing such a vital moment.

Now the chance had gone, England crashed out of the World Cup with a whimper and I looked a right knob. Happy fucking Hanukkah.

I'm pretty sure most of us have had this experience to varying degrees. Those with a dodgy Fire Stick (I see you) will know of this more than most. Sure, getting all the 3pm Saturday games is great, but what good is it if the bloody thing keeps buffering and has you screaming at the television every three seconds? Football is stressful enough.

Sometimes, there's nothing that can be done. Your internet provider has just screwed you, like Anthony Taylor at Old Trafford. But, if you do want to watch a game at home, and value your sanity, make sure you're with the most reliable internet provider for your area. It'll save you plenty of hassle in the long run. Failing that, track down the bastard who sold you the Fire Stick!

## CHANTS

Since I was a kid, I've always loved a good chant at a football match. It's one of the very few times a group of grown adults can get together, belt out an obnoxious song and it be seen as perfectly normal. Imagine trying to do that in the middle of John Lewis: 'The shop assistant's a wanker!' Singing a chant together is like being a kid again at the school carol concert and everyone changing the words to 'Jingle Bells'. 'Jingle Bells, Batman smells . . .' You remember the rest.

As a kid, I was always a fan of the basic, more puerile chants. When I first heard a whole stadium chanting, 'The referee's a wanker,' I couldn't believe it. Usually, I wasn't allowed to swear, but at football, the brakes were off. You'd see your dad belting it out, so you'd join in, whispering it under your breath, wondering if you'd be told off. Before you knew it, you were shouting it out too, your dad looking at you misty-eyed with approval. Under normal circumstances, you'd get bollocked for calling an adult a wanker. At football, it was expected.

A good chant is not only funny; it demoralises the opposition and brings the crowd together while lifting your own team. There are the favourites, like 'Who ate all the pies?', 'You're getting sacked in the morning' and the whole stadium chanting 'AAAAAH YOU'RE SHIT' when the opposition goalkeeper takes a goal kick. It's like the panto. Boo and hiss at the villains. Cheer for the heroes. Former United keeper Ben Foster has even admitted that the atmosphere at Celtic Park put him off his game in a 2008 Champions League tie. Yet, as integral as a good chant is to the match experience, it should also come with its own warning. Sing it. Enjoy it. But be fucking aware. Let's take a look at the good, the bad, and the ugly.

I've always said football fans are the wittiest bunch of pricks on the planet. So let's take a moment to pat ourselves on the back for being funny fuckers, even in the face of adversity. The following are some of my favourite chants that fans have conjured up over the years.

After John Terry was alleged to have had an affair with his teammate Wayne Bridge's girlfriend, fans chanted: 'Chelsea, wherever you may be, keep your wife from John Terry.'

Ryan Giggs was also in the firing line after having an affair with his brother's wife. This led fans to chant, 'Ryan Giggs goes to work, gives his wife two kisses, doesn't really go to work, fucks his brother's Mrs.' That's an earworm for you.

In 2008, Harry Redknapp was investigated for tax fraud. Of course, football fans didn't miss a trick, chanting, 'Stand up if you pay your tax.'

When Rio Ferdinand was banned for eight months in 2004 for missing a drug test, opposition fans chanted, to the tune of 'Rio' by Duran Duran: 'His name is Rio, and he watches from the stands.'

Emmanuel Adebayor left Arsenal in acrimonious circumstances to join Manchester City in 2009. While his replacement, Yaya Sanogo, failed to live up to expectations, a Wham-inspired chant in his honour certainly did: 'Wake me up, Yaya Sanogo, hope you're better than that cunt from Togo.' Simple but effective. Good tune. Takes down a traitor. Bigs up his replacement. Even fits in a funny swear word and some geography.

Arsenal fans also came up with another cracker in homage to their error-prone defender Emmanuel Eboué: 'Don't blame it on the sunshine. Don't blame it on the moonlight. Don't blame it on the good times. Blame it on Eboué.'

There was also this ingenious chant sung by England fans when we faced Egypt at Wembley: 'Does your mummy know you're here?' This works on so many levels.

While many of these chants have been pre-rehearsed and might last for a few games or even seasons, some of the best are made up on the spur of the moment. For instance, when a Derby fan proposed to his girlfriend at half-time, the Leeds fans chanted, 'You don't know what you're doing.'

Arsenal fans again showed their ear for a good chant during a game against Stoke at the Emirates. With Stoke 3–0 down, the PA system announced there were train delays. This inspired Arsenal fans to sing: '3–0, and you can't get home, 3–0 . . .' They don't miss a trick, those Gooners.

You don't even need to be at a game to get a chant going these days. Some of the best chants in recent years have come from a lone voice on social media, bravely offering their attempt to the masses. But be warned. It'd better be a bloody good chant, or you risk going viral for all the wrong reasons. Liverpool fans take note . . .

In 2022, one plucky young red was inspired to share a chant in homage to new signing Darwin Núñez. To the tune of 'Better Off Alone' by Alice Deejay, they sang, 'Darwin, Darwin Núñez, he came from Benfica to the big Reds, it's frightening with him and Luis Díaz. There is nobody else like

Darwin Núñez . . .' Stop! Just stop! It's making my ears bleed. It's amazing to think someone willingly put that on social media. Talk about self-harm.

Still, Liverpool fans just can't help themselves. Another shitfest appeared online to the tune of the Beatles hit 'I Feel Fine': 'Jurgen said to me, you know. We'll win the Premier League, you know. He said so! I'm in love with him, and I feel fine.' Call an ambulance! There's been a murder! Why would you do that to a Beatles song? For fuck's sake!

If there's a night school for football chants, Liverpool fans need to get on it. If not, then I'm stealing that as a business idea. Roll up. Roll up. Hear Professor Goldbridge teach Liverpool fans how to chant. Surely that's better than most reality shows around these days? Get ITV2 on the blower. We've got a hit!

Thankfully, not all fans are as bad as Liverpool at this. Some come up with some absolute crackers that not only go viral but even end up being chanted in the stadium. Sometimes, it can get even better than that. Recently, a Spurs fan posted a chant about their manager, Ange Postecoglou, to the tune of 'Angels' by Robbie Williams:

> And through it all, we'll play the way we want to, with
> big Ange Postecoglou, whether I'm right or wrong.
> It's Big Ange ball, so you can keep your Pochettino,
> Conte and Mourinho, and even Christian Gross.
> Everywhere we go, we're lovin' big Ange instead.

Bloody good that! It seems Robbie agreed as well. Soon after, he posted a video of him singing it himself. Unsurprisingly, this quickly went viral and was sung at The Tottenham Hotspur Stadium itself. Imagine how you'd feel if you were the one who'd come up with it. Stuff your gap year abroad; this is what you'll tell the grandkids about.

Unfortunately, some Neanderthals don't quite grasp what a chant is meant to do. It's meant to inspire, be funny and wind the opposition fans and players up. It's a gentle poke that invites a gentle poke back, a form of football foreplay. Done correctly, it makes the game enjoyable for both.

In the past, it wasn't unusual to see a section of fans chant racist abuse. Today, racism is very much still a problem. There are always idiots in all crowds, but I can't recall the last time you had a large section of a crowd chant racist abuse in England. These days, it's social media where racism seems to thrive. However, mocking a disaster that has rocked a club still seems acceptable in some fan's eyes. As I write this, Southampton fans have been accused of chanting about the death of Leicester's chairman in a helicopter crash, while Sheffield Wednesday fans were pictured holding up a photo of Bradley Lowery to Sunderland supporters. Fans also still think nothing of chanting about Hillsborough or the Munich disaster. This totally oversteps the mark. Thankfully, the authorities seem to be cracking down on this, with fines and even jail sentences handed out.

So, get involved with a chant, inspire your team, wind up the opposition and enjoy one of the great public communal experiences that still exists in today's society, but always remember: don't be a twat.

## HILLSBOROUGH

Football is the best sport on earth, and there's nothing quite like going to a game, but I've also experienced the flip side of the coin.

Following watching United crash out of the Cup to Forest in 1989, my dad managed to get tickets to the semi-finals. I didn't support Forest or their opponents Liverpool, but I was still keen to go. After all, this was not only a chance to spend time with my dad, but to watch a live football match. I've always loved attending football games, even if United isn't one of the teams playing. While the semi-finals of the Cup today are always held at Wembley, in 1989, the Forest–Liverpool semi-final was to be held at Sheffield Wednesday's stadium, Hillsborough.

I was excited to go; the prospect of watching Aldridge and co getting knocked out live was too good to miss. Like I said, I'd always bloody hated them, but I couldn't deny their success. In the 1980s alone, they'd already won six titles, the European Cup twice, the FA Cup once and the League Cup four times in succession. And this was a particularly good team, boasting the likes of Barnes, Rush, Aldridge and Beardsley. These were the superstars of the day, the ones all my school friends worshipped. If nothing else, I could be Billy Big Bollocks telling them I'd seen their favourite team play. Sadly, the day didn't go the way anyone had planned.

I still get flashbacks in little snippets of what happened that day. I remember standing next to my dad in the Forest end, watching the stadium fill up, both fans belting out songs, the sun shining, the feeling of a big match crackling in the air. Then, the referee blew the whistle to start the game, and a huge roar erupted around the ground. After that, the rest is almost a blur.

Around ten minutes in, I remember seeing some Liverpool fans at the opposite end scale the fences that had penned them in. While some ran onto the pitch, others approached the Forest end, gesturing wildly. I squeezed my dad's hand, afraid, thinking they were hooligans looking for a fight. (This wouldn't have been a particularly unusual thing back then. Hooliganism was the scourge of football. This was why fences had been misguidedly placed at the front of the stands to prevent fans from getting out and attacking each other or the players.)

For that reason, you can understand why most Forest fans thought the Liverpool fans were initially out for trouble. But looking towards the Leppings Lane end, I saw more and more

Liverpool fans streaming over the fences. Some even started to remonstrate with the Liverpool players on the pitch. I didn't know what was happening. I had only been to a match at a stadium a handful of times before. I had no idea if this sort of thing was normal. Suddenly, the referee blew his whistle and waved the players off.

'What's happening, Dad?' I asked.

He shook his head, apparently as baffled as I was. 'I'm not sure.'

Moments before, the crowd had been loud and boisterous. Now, it was silent. As if a spell had been cast.

I remember watching some fans rip up the wooden advertising hoardings surrounding the pitch and place another fan on top as if it were a stretcher. At this, my dad took my hand and shepherded me out of the stadium.

'Why are we leaving?' I asked.

All my dad would say is, 'The game's finished.'

We drove home in silence. Not even the radio was on, which was unusual. The only thing I remember my dad saying is he wished Forest had lost 9–0, or that the game had never happened. I still didn't understand what he meant. But no matter how much he wanted to protect me from the reality of the situation, that soon became impossible.

That night, I was sitting with my mum when the news reported that 95 fans had died at Hillsborough. None of it seemed real. As thousands of Liverpool fans had gathered outside the Leppings Lane stand before kick-off, the police panicked and opened the gates. This allowed thousands of Liverpool supporters to swarm inside. Remember, there was no numbered seating back then. All the fans were standing, so as more and more arrived from the back, those fans at the front were crushed against the fences placed to keep them in. It's too awful to comprehend. It was the blackest day in English football's history. As well as the 95 fans who died on the day or shortly afterwards, two more died years later as a result of injuries sustained that day.

Things changed pretty quickly after Hillsborough. The fences were pulled down, and the days of standing on the terraces were over. Stadiums became seating only. With the advent of Italia 90 (which we'll get into later) and then the Premier League in 1992, the culture around football also soon changed. The days of hooliganism, thankfully, came to an end. I don't think twice about taking my children to a game today. Sure, there might still be the odd idiot about, but modern stadiums and policing ensure that the vast majority of games are safe to attend.

It's strange to look back and think I was at such a horrendous event that became a watershed moment in British football history. I didn't comprehend what I was seeing at the time. Because my dad made us leave pretty quickly, I also didn't think that witnessing it did any long-term psychological damage.

However, in 2000, I attended an Oasis concert at Lansdowne Road. Out on the pitch, the crowd was like how a football crowd used to be. All standing, crammed together, and very rowdy. As more and more people pushed to get towards the stage, I suddenly had a panic attack. I felt like there was no way out. I dread to think what it was like for those Liverpool fans that day. Hillsborough was a tragedy to football that'll never be forgotten and must never happen again. No football fan should go to a football match and not come home.

You'd think that these situations had been eradicated at football grounds, particularly with the introduction of all-seater stadiums and no more fences. Yet, in recent years, we've seen signs that there are still problems. In the 2022 Champions League final in Paris, Liverpool fans faced another frightening ordeal when the entrances to the stadium became dangerously overcrowded. There were even issues at Hillsborough again in January 2023, when Newcastle played Sheffield Wednesday in the FA Cup. Despite the Leppings Lane end now being all-seater and the fences having long been pulled down, Newcastle fans complained of severe overcrowding.

So, even today, if you go to a game, always be on the lookout for danger or overcrowding issues. Report anything that looks untoward. It could save your life, as well as many others.

# 5

# TAKE CONTROL

Have you ever recorded yourself commentating on a Subbuteo game and then sent the tape to a mate? I can feel the tumbleweeds rushing past my face. I appreciate it's not for everyone. It's a refined taste, like Neil Warnock, but as a kid, I somehow fell into this weird arrangement. Let me explain.

When I was nine, I got a Subbuteo set for Christmas. What's that? I hear younger readers cry. It was basically a green mat, set out like a football pitch, where you could flick little players with your fingers at the ball. I know. It sounds shit, but we didn't have *FIFA*, alright! And I wasn't the only one who liked it. They used to sell over 300,000 sets a year, so check yourself before you wreck yourself.

Anyway, the Subbuteo set I got for Christmas was majestic. Dragging my mum out of bed at five in the morning, I rushed downstairs to find that, like Amazon Prime, Santa had well and truly fucking delivered. There it was, the crème de la crème of Subbuteo sets. Not only did it come with a pitch and four teams, but also a stand and bloody floodlights. My fucking God. My auntie and uncle also bought me the Subbuteo Man United team, which had me salivating more than a basset hound over a steak.

For a long time, I was happy to play by myself, taking turns flicking the ball for each team while munching through packs of Midget Gems. This might sound boring to some, but I was totally engrossed. To me, this was as good as the real thing. What I particularly enjoyed was commentating as I played. 'Robson sprays a long ball forward to Hughes. He hits it first time. GOAL!' 'What a strike by Hughes. The crowd is going crazy . . .' You get the idea. My family probably thought I was a right little weirdo. I'd even stand in front of the mirror for hours afterwards doing my post-match analysis. In the end, my stepmother told my father that I was being too loud and my poor stepbrother wasn't getting a chance. You run with the big dogs; that's what happens, I'm afraid. It's sink or swim, my friend. Little did I know that this was all perfect training for *The United Stand* in years to come.

I played Subbuteo for years, well into secondary school. By that time, I'd amassed quite a collection of teams. My favourite was the 1993 United away team, with Brian McClair leading the line, but I was also partial to the Norwich set, as the yellow kits had three green Adidas stripes down it. The Arsenal 'bruised banana' was epic as well.

After years of practice, I thought I was pretty good, but it wasn't as if I ever faced any real competition. My friends and family would have the odd game with me, but they hadn't spent hours honing their flick craft, nor did they appreciate the seriousness of the game. At best, it was a token effort. I had no idea there were Subbuteo leagues back then. If I had known and been able to go, that would have been my life. It's probably for the best I missed out. I was weird enough. But then, something miraculous happened.

When I was in secondary school, I heard a rumour (not the Richard Gere or Prince ones) that another kid was also a Subbuteo nerd. For the first time in my life, I found someone who was equally committed. We were like the Spider-Man meme, pointing at each other. *I see you too, you right little weirdo.* For our first meeting, we organised a secret meet-up in the playground. The cool kids smoked fags behind the bike shed. We talked about Subbuteo. We lived in different towns and there was no chance we could bring our stuff in to school, so we couldn't actually play each other for real, so we came up with another bonkers idea. We decided to set up a league, playing against ourselves while also recording ourselves commentating on a tape recorder. The next day, we'd swap our tapes in the playground for the other to listen to. Don't judge me, alright. I'm coming clean here. This was a top-secret operation. We knew that if news got out, we'd be ostracised. We were a Mark Bosnich and Dwight Yorke sex tape waiting to happen.

I thought we'd already pushed the boat out, but my man took things to another level. One day, he gave me a tape, and he had somehow overlaid real crowd noise over his commentating. It blew my mind. I had to do the same. By the end, our Subbuteo tapes sounded as good as any real game. Ultimately, I think my commentary was better. I mean, where is he today? Exactly. Sometimes, the big victories in life take time. Enjoy them when they come.

Sadly, like all good childhood pursuits, my Subbuteo days gradually came to an end. It's no coincidence that this happened around 1994 when the first *FIFA* computer game was released on Mega Drive. I also have no idea what happened to my Subbuteo set. I suppose some fucker binned it or gave it away to charity. Heartless bastards.

Every so often, I'll come across an epic Subbuteo set on eBay, complete with stadium and floodlights, and be sorely tempted to treat myself. But I never pull the trigger. I know it would be so bad compared to *FIFA*. I'm better off cherishing the memories and remembering all the good times. However, after this trip down memory lane, I've found that Subbuteo leagues are still a thing, and there's even a World Cup tournament coming up in Tunbridge Wells. Who's up for a *United Stand* Subbuteo watch-along as I dust off my skills against the world's best?

As liberating as it has been to get this story off my chest, there is actually a wider point to this. Any therapist would have a field day working out why I became so obsessed with Subbuteo. Looking back now, it's pretty simple. It was all about having some sort of control over the game. Far too often, it feels as if we put our emotions into the hands of our team and hope for the best. There's a certain thrill to that, and it's one of the reasons football is so popular and infuriating. Yet as I found with my foray into the world of Subbuteo, there are plenty of ways that us fans can exert some control over the game. Some madder than others . . .

## PRE-MATCH SUPERSTITIONS

Before every game at Euro 96, Gazza held Les Ferdinand's balls for luck. It's true. I'm not just making shit up. Look it up. Feel silly now, don't you? With 'Three Lions' echoing in the background, Les would patiently wait by the changing room door with his pants down while Gazza took his family jewels in his hand, or two hands by the sound of it . . . Anyway, it certainly did the trick, as Gazza was fantastic. Thank you, Les, for your sacrifice.

Superstition is a big thing in football. Paul Ince had to be last out of the tunnel and wouldn't put his shirt on until he made his way onto the pitch. Before kick-off, Laurent Blanc would always kiss Fabien Barthez's bald head. This might have helped win France the World Cup, but the same routine did fuck all when they both played for United. Meanwhile,

Alan Shearer always ate chicken and beans before any game, propelling him to goal-scoring glory and leaving an empty seat next to him on the team bus. But superstition isn't just for players. Fans get involved as well.

A lot of this is standard stuff, which we've all done from time to time. Some have to sit on the same part of the sofa, while others need to kiss the club badge before kick-off. There are even those who refuse to watch a game with someone they think is 'unlucky'. Judging by how United has done in recent years, maybe I should stop watching games with you lot. Bunch of Jonahs, the lot of you! Amazingly, many fans believe that their ritual has affected a game's outcome.

As crazy as this sounds, there is some method to the madness. There's a theory called the Butterfly Effect, which rests on the notion that the world is deeply interconnected. One small act can influence something miles away, like if a butterfly flaps its wings, it might help create a tornado weeks later. Everything we do, no matter how small, affects the world. It's quite a stretch to think a lucky jumper will directly help your team win, but why take the risk? I'm certainly a big believer in all of this.

When I was a kid, I became convinced that if I walked out of a room, it might affect the game. The most memorable time this happened to me was during England vs West Germany in the semi-final of the 1990 World Cup. I was watching the game at home and was absolutely bursting for a wee. Still, I refused to move. I was totally convinced England wouldn't score if I left. Even if I had to piss myself on the sofa in front of all my family, I wasn't going to budge. Sweating, holding my legs together, and bouncing up and down, I was in it until the death.

Just as a trickle squeezed out Paul Parker played a long ball over the West German defence, for Gary Lineker to volley home the equaliser. I claimed the assist for that one. If I had gone to the toilet, we wouldn't have scored. I deserved a place on the open-top bus. I was a national bloody hero. That's how I felt anyway. But where's my medal? Hey? Like a receiver in a porno, I'd played my part.

Insanity like this makes you feel connected to the game. You're not just a fan watching on the sofa. You're a secret weapon. The ultimate good luck charm. Don't laugh. England managers have done far more bonkers things. In the run-up to the 1998 World Cup, Glenn Hoddle famously employed a faith healer called Eileen Drewery to help the players. When Eileen touched Ray Parlour's head to heal an injury, he jokingly said, 'A short back and sides while you're there.' Well played, Ray. Although this came at a cost. Because of this, Parlour didn't play for England under Hoddle again and even missed out on the World Cup. Still, if it's any consolation, Ray, it was a good one. If you'd gone to the World Cup, would you have played? Probably not, so at least you got a good gag out of it in the long run.

Yet this just emphasises my point. Football clubs employ a number of physios, analysts, doctors, faith healers, you name it, to give the players an edge. Why shouldn't a fan trying not to piss his pants to give his team some good luck not also be a key member of staff? If an England manager can believe in faith healers, then fans have every right to believe they can make a difference. So, Gareth Southgate, I'm fit and available for the Euros. I'll take my seat next to you in the dugout and won't move, even if I have to piss myself on national television. Worst-case scenario, it makes for great entertainment. Stuff *I'm a Celebrity*. Watch Goldbridge neck a litre of water and try not to piss his pants on the England bench instead. At least it would keep Nick Pope entertained.

The world works in mysterious ways. Maybe we really are in the Matrix. Maybe the machines controlling us have secretly picked out a glitch that ensures a certain team wins if someone on earth follows a certain rule. Maybe we're all in Harry Maguire's simulation, and he's picked a life where he gets to play for Manchester United. Listen, it's a long shot, but why take the risk? Do whatever you need to do to make your team win. Just don't expect any thanks for it.

## BECOME A MANAGER

Forget the darker, later years, where José Mourinho went all in as a Bond villain. Despite all that nonsense, he's still one of the greatest managers in the history of the game. However, before embarking on his managerial career, he had no great background in football. In fact, his playing career was limited at best.

Predominantly playing in the Belenenses reserve team, he only got called up to the first team when his father was named manager. Even then, he rarely played. Even when his father tried to bring him on, the club president overruled him! This is the Mourinho origin story. You won't let my own father pick me! I'll show you, ya bunch of pricks!

With his playing career behind him, Mourinho moved into coaching, initially taking a job at a local school. Then, almost out of nowhere, he got his big break. In 1992, with Mourinho able to speak Portuguese and English and having some background in football, he applied to work as Bobby Robson's translator at Sporting Lisbon. He got the job and, for the next four years, followed Sir Bobby like a faithful hound to Porto and then Barcelona. During this time, they built a close relationship, with Mourinho able to share his views on football. It's fair to say Sir Bobby was impressed. So much so that he soon allowed his translator to take some first-team coaching sessions. It sounds bonkers, but Sir Bobby clearly realised Mourinho had something about him.

With a taste for coaching, Mourinho quickly ditched the translating gig. In 2000 he got the manager's job at Benfica, but it was at Porto where his managerial career really ignited. In 2003 he won the UEFA Cup and then in 2004 the

Champions League, knee-sliding like a right prick at Old Trafford in the process. The so-called 'Special One' has now won 26 major trophies and counting. Still, let us never forget that he says one of his best achievements is finishing second in the league at United. When you have Phil Jones and Chris Smalling in your team, you have to agree.

Mourinho is far from the only football fan who watched their team and thought, *Fuck this, I'm better than Steve Kean. And I'll prove it.* But for most of us, it's sadly only a pipe dream. If you're middle-aged, well-entrenched in your career and have no background in professional football whatsoever, you've more chance of winning the lottery than becoming a professional football manager. Unless you're Mark Warburton. Take a seat. This is one of my all-time favourite football stories.

Warburton played some non-league football in the 1980s before becoming a high-flying currency trader in the City. However, as he reached his early forties, he, like many of us do, began reassessing his life. While most of us men buy skinny jeans, drink hipster beers and experiment with facial hair, Warburton had an urge for a career in football. He certainly thought he could do a better job than most of the managers he watched. Despite having a family to support, he decided to take the plunge. Quitting his job, he took coaching courses and then travelled around Europe, watching coaching sessions at Sporting CP, Ajax, Valencia, Barcelona and Willem

II. Eventually, he got a job coaching the youth teams at Watford until he was appointed academy manager in 2006. After becoming sporting director at Brentford in 2011, he was finally appointed first-team manager in 2013, leading the club to promotion to the Championship in his first season in charge. Since then, Warburton has managed Rangers, Nottingham Forest and QPR.

It just goes to show that if you're fed up with how your team is doing and want to take control of things yourself, what's stopping you from getting your coaching badges and channelling your inner Mourinho? A word of warning, though. It's not as easy as it looks.

Over the last few years, I've been lucky enough to manage a team in the annual Sidemen Charity Match. Both teams are made up of social media stars, and it has been a phenomenal experience. It's allowed me to stand on the touchline at the Valley, and then West Ham's Olympic Stadium, and hear 60,000 fans chant, 'Goldbridge! Goldbridge!' At least, that's what I think they were chanting . . . I'm sure the word 'wanker' wasn't used once . . . Still, it was a great experience. However, even though it was supposed to be a bit of fun, I also found it very pressurised. You suddenly realise that everyone's eyes are on you. You can hear murmurings and grumblings from the crowd when you make a substitution. When you step into the technical area to make a change, you know everyone is analysing and dissecting what you're doing. You can't even pick your fucking nose. Although, saying that, it didn't stop Germany manager Joachim Löw from touching his knob on the touchline and then smelling his fingers. He then repeated the trick with his bum. I suppose when you've won the World Cup, you can do what you like. Nevertheless, it's something I won't be trying. No matter how many clicks it would get.

When you're in front of 60,000 fans in the stadium, you realise everyone has opinions – but, ultimately, it all falls down to you. And if you fuck it up, thousands of people are going to see just what a useless prick you really are. During the second charity game, I particularly felt the pressure when we picked up a lot of injuries. Through no fault of anyone's, we were suddenly in disarray, and I felt helpless. At one point, I was worried we would get pumped 20 nil! Thankfully, with a few tactical tweaks and some good luck, we managed to steady the ship and save me from looking like a total prat.

I can't imagine how football managers cope with this level of pressure every single game. It's no wonder Graeme Souness, Gérard Houllier and Joe Kinnear developed heart problems. It's an adrenalin rush, but it certainly takes its toll. After these games, I was exhausted. I can't imagine having to pick myself up, get into training the next day and do it all over again a few days later.

Over the years, I've enjoyed managing my daughter's U-12s team, and I've also had a few amateur teams ask me to get involved. Sadly, my work with *The United Stand* is all-consuming. Yet, as I get older, I'd love to emulate my grandad, managing a Saturday afternoon team, getting into a changing room smelling of deep heat and preparing the team for battle. It would certainly beat United fucking up my weekends every week. Either way, if you just can't face watching another highly paid manager deliver another disasterclass, what's stopping you from taking their place?

## FANTASY FOOTBALL

As you might imagine, after my foray into the Subbuteo world, I was an early adopter of Fantasy Football. This allowed me to really gain control over the game and then some.

It first came to the UK in 1994 when it was introduced by the *Daily Telegraph*. With a circulation of 950,000 readers, it's estimated that more than 350,000 people signed up to play and ruined their lives forever in the process. Back then, you had to pick your team from the back of the newspaper, fill in a form and post it off. Despite this being a total ball ache, we didn't know any better. Every week, you'd eagerly look at the leaderboard published in the paper and hope your name was there. There were no weekly transfers, though. In fact, there were none at all. If your star player got injured in the first game of the season and was out for months, then you were screwed. For that reason, you were bloody stupid if you picked Darren Anderton. He wasn't called 'Sick Note' for nothing, let me tell you.

Even when you could finally make transfers or change your lineup, you had to do so by phone. This was all well and good but added a new problem to contend with. Before the days of social media, finding out a team's likely starting lineup was far more difficult and could play havoc with your selection. However, one Fantasy Football lunatic got around this with a stroke of ingenuity.

Tim Benson was so dedicated to his cause that he used to pose as a journalist on Friday afternoons and would call up clubs, asking for an interview with the assistant manager. Now this was where he was being a right clever clogs. No one ever wanted to interview the assistant manager, so they had verbal diarrhoea when Tim was on the phone. Lulled into a false sense of security, Benson would then skilfully prise the next day's lineup from them with all the tact of a butcher persuading a cow that becoming a steak was in its best interest. With this knowledge, he would call Fantasy Football HQ and confirm his team. Tim, I doff my cap to you, sir. This is magnificent dedication. Even real managers don't show such commitment to the cause. Come to think of it, why isn't Erik ten Hag doing this?

'Errrr hello, I am a journalist and I . . .'

'You sound like that bloke who manages United, y'know . . .'

'I . . . oh fuck . . . wrong number.'

Fantasy Football is, of course, a different beast today. It's obviously far more interactive. There are multiple opportunities for transfers and the ability to be in leagues with your friends or work colleagues, often with big prize money up for grabs. The only problem with this is that picking and managing a team becomes all-consuming. It's not like the old days, where once you sent off your team your work was done for the season. Now, you can constantly tinker with players and formations, like Mikel Arteta, with an army of stats at your disposal to supposedly help or drive you crazy. Every day is like a scene from *Moneyball*.

When I worked in an office, I would spend most of my day managing my fantasy team, flipping between screens whenever I heard my boss coming. (C'mon. I know you've done it as well. Don't play all innocent with me.) I'd spend hours working out which Swansea player I could get dirt cheap or who might get me a few points from the bench. Like going with a mate's ex, the big ethical decision was always if I could really justify putting a City or Liverpool player in my team. Sure, they'd get me a few points, but then I'd have to cheer for my rivals. It just felt wrong. Could I really look myself in the mirror if I put Gerrard in my team and made him captain? Of course, I could. I'm a winner, me. Come on, Gerrard, you great big fucking red you. Come to Goldbridge FC.

For a period, Fantasy Football totally took over my life. I'd stay up late at night, agonising over whether to play my wildcard. I took it really fucking seriously. One year, I even finished in the top 100 in the country. See, I'm not just all mouth. Let's see Pep do that. But in the end, I had to take a step away for my own sanity. The straw that broke the camel's back was the introduction of Friday night kick-offs. This killed me. My routine used to involve spending Saturday mornings trawling over social media for any useful stats or last-minute injury news and then submitting my team before the midday deadline. When Friday kick-offs became a thing, it became impossible to focus on work, as I'd be trying to research my team all day. If work got in the way, my team would be a mess. That would totally ruin my weekend. Unless I could fully devote myself to the team, I knew I wasn't doing myself just-ice. I knew how Kevin Keegan felt when he walked away from managing England in 2000.

It takes incredible dedication and skill to win the Fantasy Football title. These people must live like monks. Living it. Breathing it. You can't have a life. But don't think of Fantasy Football as a waste of time. Far from it. As I said, it helps some of us feel like we have ownership and control over the game. It also encourages you to follow teams other than your own and support their players, and get some joy out of a Luton player getting you an assist. Without Fantasy Football, you might never even know these players existed. Best of all, if you're really good at it, it might not only win you a big chunk of money – the winner nets around £250,000 – but lead to a change of career.

This is what happened to economist Rui Marques. With a gift for stats and a vast football knowledge, the Portuguese football fan entered the *Daily Mirror* Fantasy Football competition for the 2009/10 season and won the £75,000 first prize. The next year, he did it again, entering *Bild*'s competition in Germany and taking away €100,000. By now, professional clubs were taking note of this Fantasy Football prodigy. He soon began scouting for Portuguese clubs before becoming a European scout at Sporting Kansas City in the United States and then with Polish champions Legia Warsaw. So, what are you waiting for? That team isn't going to pick itself!

If you're thinking that Fantasy Football is just a game and no match for the real thing, you could not be more wrong. In 2008, non-league Ebbsfleet United played fantasy football for real when it was taken over by MyFootballClub. This con- sisted of a consortium of thousands of football fans who each stumped up an annual fee of £35 to take charge of the club. They not only sanctioned transfers and kit designs but chose the team online each week.

Amazingly, things started off very well. In its first year under its new ownership Ebbsfleet won the FA Trophy and finished a respectable 11th place in the Conference. However, despite this initial success, interest from the fans began to wane, as did their annual £35 subscriptions. Soon, Ebbsfleet was battling financial issues and, after being relegated to Conference South, the club was sold. Still, the club enjoyed one of its most successful seasons the year the fans were in charge.

## FIFA

I used to love the eighties film *The Last Starfighter*. It told the story of a kid who was the best in the world at an arcade video game. Little did he know that the game was really a test to see who was good enough to join an intergalactic fleet. I like to think that this is really what *FIFA* is. Top football clubs are secretly monitoring the game for the next up-and-coming manager. I love playing it regardless, but there's always a voice deep inside me that thinks, *I need to be at my best today, someone at United might be watching.*

I first took gaming seriously when playing *Championship Manager* in the nineties. I received it as a present one Christmas and didn't come up for air until January. I barely slept. I was on it 24/7, dragging Walsall to the Champions League. It's the type of thing you should really put on your CV. Sepp Hedel, a superfan of the game's spin-off and successor, *Football Manager*, was so obsessed that he played more than 333 seasons from 2017 to 2019 and won close to 1,000 trophies, earning himself a place in the *Guinness Book of Records*.

While I adored *Championship Manager*, it was *FIFA* that really got its claws into me. Not only was it the most realistic football game ever created, but if United lost a game to West Ham in real life, I could just load up *FIFA* and replay the fixture until I gave those dirty Hammers the beating they deserved. It was not only fun but also a form of therapy. Have some of that, Harry Redknapp. You're not singing songs about sucking off Michael Jackson's ex-monkey now, are you!

While I have always pretty much played *FIFA* alone, I was forced to bring myself to wider attention in 2020, when the COVID-19 pandemic caused the football season to be put indefinitely on hold. Suddenly, I was faced with trying to run a football YouTube channel with no football to report on. Out of sheer desperation, I decided to livestream myself playing *FIFA*. I had no idea how people would respond to this. It seems people were either more bored than I thought, or they really bought into my buccaneering style of play. Think Kevin Keegan's Newcastle with a dash of Brazil circa 2002.

One Tuesday afternoon, more than 25,000 people watched me play in the European Cup final. That's more than the average attendance at most Championship clubs and ten times the number of genuine Man City fans in existence today. This was so successful that it has since become a regular feature, and I get hundreds of thousands of views every time I play. If any football clubs are out there looking for a manager to bring the crowds back with a brand of exciting, attacking football, and plenty of swearing at the opposition, you know where to find me.

In 2015, following the dismissal of Brendan Rodgers from Liverpool, *FIFA* enthusiast Adam Kneale applied for the managerial vacancy. He even got a response from the Chief Executive:

Dear Mr Kneale,

Thank you for your recent enquiry in relation to the current vacant position as First Team Manager at Liverpool Football Club.

Unfortunately, we are unable to process your interest at this time as we are looking for someone with more experience in the professional game. In relation to the experience that you have provided, taking Portsmouth Football Club from the 2nd Division and going on to winning the Premier League and the Champions League in four seasons on *FIFA 15*, it is not the required standard of experience that we are looking for at this time.

However, we thank you for your interest, and we look forward to hearing from you in the future.

Yours sincerely,

Ian Ayre

Chief Executive

To be fair, the club eventually appointed Jürgen Klopp, so they probably got that decision right. Yet, if Mick McCarthy and Mark Hughes can keep getting jobs, there's no reason a *FIFA* champion shouldn't throw their hat into the ring, too.

Even if the big clubs aren't paying attention to our exploits on *FIFA*, big business is: esports have become hugely popular in recent years. If you're good enough, you can compete on *FIFA* on behalf of your club, in competitions that are streamed online or even in arenas in front of thousands of fans. According to Statista, the global esports market revenue is expected to grow to $1.62 billion by 2025, with the audience projected to be 577 million. Playing *FIFA* in an arena, with millions of fans watching and cheering you on, sounds better than being a footballer. You get the same rush and adulation without needing to keep fit and watch what you eat. Someone get Eden Hazard on the phone.

## SET UP YOUR OWN CLUB

A lot of fans had a bad feeling when the Glazers took over Manchester United in 2005, like when you microwave that cottage pie that's been knocking around the fridge for a week. It just smelt dodgy. Some fans were so fucked off they organised protests; others stopped going to Old Trafford. And a few were so pissed off they set up an entirely new football club altogether.

FC United of Manchester was started by a disgruntled group of United fans sick and tired of the way modern football was going. Starting off in the North West Counties Football League, the club has since risen through the divisions and is now in English football's seventh tier – its peak came in 2015–19, when the club reached the dizzy heights of the National League North.

FC United is far from the only club that has been set up by pissed-off fans who want to enjoy some success. In 2003 Wimbledon controversially moved from south London to Milton Keynes and rebranded itself as MK Dons. What a load of shit that is. Unsurprisingly, a lot of Wimbledon fans weren't too pleased with having 100 years of tradition flushed down the toilet, especially as Milton Keynes is 80 miles north up the M1. How did the FA allow this to happen? Who was in charge, the bloody Chuckle Brothers? Still, it could have been even worse. At one stage, former owner Sam Hammam had looked into possibly relocating the club to Dublin or even Dubai! It's no wonder that a group of Wimbledon fans were so fucked off they decided to set up a new club: AFC Wimbledon. MK

Dons kept its place in the league, but AFC Wimbledon had to start again, right at the bottom.

Over the years, AFC Wimbledon has worked its way up the football pyramid and been promoted six times, reaching the Football League for the first time in 2011 and eventually League One in 2016. In 2012, as luck would have it, AFC Wimbledon was drawn in the FA Cup third round to face hated rivals MK Dons. More than 3,000 AFC Wimbledon fans made the journey to Milton Keynes, many wearing contamination suits as a form of protest. MK Dons might have won that particular encounter 2–1, thanks to a last-minute goal, but in the 2016/17 season, when AFC Wimbledon was promoted to League One, the club finally met MK Dons in a league game. This time, Wimbledon emerged victorious, swiping their hated rivals aside with a 2–0 victory. Have some of that justice jam on toast.

The demise of Wimbledon also became the inspiration for another fan-owned club, which is perhaps the most bonkers story of them all. In 1999, with Wimbledon relegated from the Premier League and looking to relocate, one fan had had enough. Rather than continue to travel and support Wimbledon, Marc White decided to manage a park's team instead. Setting up Dorking Wanderers FC, he entered his new club in the fifth tier of the Crawley & District League. This was no semi-pro setup, with a sugar daddy or crowdfunding throwing money at it. Money was tight. The club played on a council-owned pitch and the players still had to pay their £5 subs. It was football right at the bottom. But White was a man on a mission. He had his eyes on greater things. -

After 12 promotions in 23 years, White has led his team to the National League, just one level below the Football League. Throughout the journey, he's been a player, chairman and manager. The club even has a youth system, with more than 1,150 kids involved, and it has also become the heart of the local community, with locals wearing replica Dorking kits. Marc White took the plunge and is living the dream. It sounds bloody hard work, but what's stopping any fan from doing the same? Set up a team. Start at the bottom. Dream big.

## START A FAN CHANNEL

It was 2014. I was married, had two young kids, and worked for the police on the economic crime team. I was happy with my lot. Life was good. It wasn't necessarily my dream job, but I had worked hard to get there and liked the people I worked with. At the very least, it paid the bills. I certainly wasn't looking for a change in career. As far as I was concerned, if I stayed where I was and kept working my way up the ladder, I'd be happy. In a footballing sense I was James

Ward-Prowse: talented, content, capable of bigger things and under-appreciated. Then, an idea slapped me across the face like a big wet salmon.

It's weird how life's big moments come along when you least expect them. The smallest thought can suddenly blossom into something that takes you in a totally different direction. My moment came in the swimming pool during a family holiday. While the kids were playing, and I had a moment to myself, I focused on the other big thing in my life: Manchester United. I daydreamed about how Louis van Gaal could bring back the glory days, if he wasn't being hamstrung by the Glazers. I suddenly became frustrated. I knew that plenty of other fans felt the same as me. I just wished there was a space where we could all share our thoughts together.

Twitter was around then, but it wasn't the beast it would become. For most football fans, communication was all about forums. My favourite was the BBC's 606. Every day, I'd log into the Manchester United section and share posts with fellow fans about the state of the team and the direction of the club. It was like a secret society where a few thousand of us could gather and talk football. The only problem was it wasn't instantaneous. I'd post something, then keep refreshing the page, waiting for a response. The only other way to get your voice out there as a fan was by ringing radio shows like *606* or talkSPORT. I loved all that. They allowed fans to vent and circumnavigate the pundits, whose opinions held a lot of weight. But I found that even this was limited. Sure, it got your voice out there, but you weren't really having a conversation with fellow fans of your club or grouping together. Then, it hit me. What if there was a Manchester United fan channel on YouTube? Wouldn't it be great if you could livestream yourself and a couple of mates talking about United, and viewers could make comments, ask questions and interact? This wasn't a revolutionary idea in itself. At the time, there were other fan channels on YouTube, but, by and large, they were owned by TV companies. For me, they didn't feel authentic. Certainly not for what I had in mind. They were too slick and well edited. Fans of those clubs might have been on camera, but they were still spewing out similar stuff to what you'd get on Sky and the BBC. As far as I could tell, there wasn't an independent fan channel out there. Just as I started to run away with myself, my kids called out to me. For now, my daydreaming was over.

This was all just a seed of an idea that lasted no more than a few seconds. We have plenty of these in a lifetime. Most don't stick. But something about this one did. While I was soon back playing with the kids, I casually mentioned the idea to my wife that night. It was a way of putting it out there into the world to see how it sounded out loud. The more I spoke, the more I felt I was on to something. My wife certainly didn't shoot me down. She thought it sounded like a good idea. She had consumed a lot of sangria though.

When I returned home, I floated the idea to a few mates whom I'd met online and who were also United supporters: Martin, Rich, Alex and Kev. They were all up for it. It wasn't like this was a big thing at the time. It wouldn't cost a lot of money to do, and all we intended to do was just get online and chat about United after we had put the kids to bed on a Sunday night. It was just supposed to be a bit of fun. Nothing more than a hobby, really, like Gareth Bale playing for Real Madrid. Everyone was enthusiastic, but there was a small problem. None of us was that technically minded. We'd certainly never livestreamed before. But after some research, we didn't think it would be that hard. So, one Sunday night, four of us put our kids to bed, sat in front of a computer, switched on our webcams and chatted about the latest issues affecting the team. If I remember rightly, I think I cocked on about Fellaini being shit. Start as you mean to go on, Mark. Take no prisoners. No one leaves alive.

Unsurprisingly, we had no idea what we were doing. It's not as if you could go to university to learn this stuff at the time or that it was even a conceivable career path back then. We just had to make it up as we went along. As you might expect, it was raw and a bit all over the place. I think we had a grand total of six people watching for that first show. That included the four of us, so there were just two random people out there who had somehow found the stream. It's a bit shite, really, isn't it? We might have been disappointed with this and consigned the idea to the bin, but whatever the viewing figures were, we had enjoyed ourselves, even if barely anyone else had – a bit like watching *Call the Midwife*.

Every Sunday night, we kept logging on and slowly began to hone our craft. If nothing else, it gave us an outlet to vent and put our thoughts into the world. I certainly felt better for doing so. Slowly but surely, our audience also started to grow through nothing more than word of mouth. I remember one day, while we were live, one of us messaged the others to say that 96 people were watching! I thought we had made it. I really did.

Other 'fan channels' used to pre-record ten-minute shows and would then stick them on YouTube. Because our show was live, we sort of innovated the live content football scene on YouTube. It wasn't just people logging on to watch us talk. It was clear they loved being able to interact at the same time. It made the audience feel part of something.

We started to do more content, and our viewing figures kept on growing. Finally, after a year or so, I had taken the concept as far as I could. Trying to work a full-time job while juggling making YouTube content was becoming more difficult. It was clear that our viewers wanted more, and I was struggling to find the time to give it to them. I'd be preparing and recording content all night, and then I'd have to go to work all day. I was dead. No use to anybody. Like Kalvin

Phillips at City. Something had to give. I had to make a decision. Quit my job and go full-time, or stop.

As successful as *The United Stand* was at the time, we weren't making any money. That had never been the point of it, though. Like I said, it was just supposed to be a bit of fun. But I had seen it could be more than that. However, going full-time was a huge risk. I had a family to support. It was like Eric Dier telling everyone he was really a centre back, then hoping for the best. If it went wrong, it could go Eric Dier wrong. I wasn't just a young kid, living at home, making content and hoping something might come of it. I was 34. I had real responsibilities. Life could get very difficult if things didn't work out. It also wasn't as if I could talk to many people about it either. That's the thing with crazy dreams. Most people won't get it, and certainly if there's nothing they can judge it against. As I said, back then, independent fan channels were very much in their infancy. Trying to turn a fledgling show into a full-time career, especially when I was a 34-year-old dad of two kids, seemed insane to most people.

But the thing is, while I had previously been quite happy plodding along in my job, now I had opened a new door, and I didn't want to shut it. Thankfully, I found a sensible solution. I asked my boss if I could take a six-month sabbatical. I was honest. I explained what I hoped to do and the risks it involved. Fair play to him. It would have been easy for him to shoot me down, but he agreed to keep my job open for me. This took an enormous amount of pressure off, although it was now replaced by a new kind. I had six months to make this work. Thankfully, it seemed that the harder I worked, the more viewers I got, and the channel kept growing and growing. And it was during this time that I also came across a new concept to take things to another level.

When I first started out, I'd watch a game by myself and tweet as I watched. After the game, I'd then do a match reaction video. But there was a problem with this. While I was tweeting, I was missing chunks of the bloody game. That's when I had a brainwave. A live watch-along. I'd watch the game and stream myself as I watched. It seems so simple now, but no one else did this back then. Not the way we did it anyway. Sky used to have *Fanzone*, which was basically two rival fans watching a game together and commentating as their teams played each other. It was good fun, but other fans couldn't interact with it as they watched. Then there was *Gogglebox*. On the face of it, the concept seemed crazy: people watching other people's reactions as they watched TV. It was as if we had jumped the shark. Yet, it was an enormously popular programme. Putting all this together, I thought football watch-alongs could be a thing. Pat yourself on the back, Mark! You were bloody right.

While I'm sure people tune in for my tactical insight into the game, the chat box has also become a big feature. Sure, we get into the football, but where else can you see a pundit asked the question: what would you do if your girlfriend pooed the bed? I'd like to see Neville and Carragher debate that one!

I still can't believe this is my job. I get to watch and talk about Manchester United alongside fans from all over the world. For me, it's a dream. When I was a kid, I used to commentate and give interviews to myself on my Subbuteo games. Now I get to do it for real. Although sometimes I do wake up in the morning and see clips of me losing my shit going viral, and think, *You look a right bloody prat there.* It's also difficult to stream from home at times. I've had my wife switch the football over to *Strictly Come Dancing* midstream, as well as my kids putting on *Peppa Pig.* Again, you don't see Gary Lineker stomping out of the studio to tell his kids to keep the noise down.

The watch-along has, in fact, been so popular that other fan channels have ripped it off. Don't think I don't see you! To be fair, some are decent imitations. Others are like watching Mr Bean's cousin. All the gear and no idea. They're like those rip-off KFC places you see on every high street these days. You might be selling chicken, but it's not the Colonel.

Anyway, all of this led to me finally receiving ad revenue from YouTube. I even managed to attract a few sponsors. It wasn't much, but the fact that I had proven this idea could be monetised gave me the belief that things were going in the right direction. When my six months were up, I certainly wasn't making as much as I had been in my job. Yet I knew I couldn't stop now. It was all-or-nothing time. Do or die. It was still a massive risk, but it was time to go all in, like Rain Man in the casino, except I wasn't counting cards. Fair play to Mrs Goldbridge. She was very supportive. I might not have had the balls to do it without her, but she's been with me every step of the way.

Going full-time was the best decision I've ever made. Don't get me wrong, it was still tough at times. I was doing this alone. If I needed a break, I couldn't take one. I just had to keep on grinding, no matter where I was. There's one particularly funny moment in the early days when I was on a family holiday in Mallorca. While I took the kids to the beach, I thought I could quickly fit in a video discussing United's latest links to James Rodríguez. I should have known better. As I started doing a livestream, a man selling pineapples came into the picture.

'You want some pineapple?'

I tried to focus on the camera, but he asked again. 'Hey, you want pineapple?'

I smiled and kept looking at the camera. 'I'm live to a couple of thousand people here, mate.'

Suddenly, he pulled out his pineapple carving knife and pointed it towards me. 'You a wanker.'

I had to cut the stream short to avoid being stabbed. I think some people thought I had set it all up, but that was honestly what had happened. Still, the video quickly went viral, so at least there was that. A word of warning, though: don't buy fruit in Mallorca.

These days, we have hundreds of thousands of views per video. Some even go into the millions. I know for a fact we get way more views than a national newspaper on a daily basis or a national radio station. We probably get more than some national TV stations as well. It's no wonder that some mainstream broadcasters have treated us with contempt. I get it. It's like coming home and catching your partner having a good time with someone else. But you know what, maybe you should have treated them to a game of Monopoly every now and again? At times some of them have been an absolute bunch of shithouses. It was as if a real fan, just being themselves, was an affront. While we might never be accepted by some, I'm happy to say that attitudes are slowly changing. In 2022 I was even asked to present a weekly show on talk-SPORT. This was a dream come true. I still get to work on *The United Stand*, but I also have a chance to speak to an audience on Britain's most popular sports radio broadcaster. Sometimes I have to pinch myself. However, even this has come with its challenges.

When I was first asked to do the show, I didn't think it would be possible. I'm based in Birmingham, and there was talk of me driving up and down to London. I was dead keen to do it, but like Christmas pudding after a large Christmas dinner, I just didn't know how I could fit everything in. Then, there was a meeting of great minds, and we came to a solution. I could do the show from home like I do with *The United Stand*. Of course, it didn't go as planned. This is the honest to God truth. On the first bloody show, the broadband went down an hour before I was due on air. Nothing I could do would get the fucker working. I felt like a porn star, getting screwed from all angles. My internet was as useful as Stephen Hawkins's treadmill before and after he died. An absolute shitshow. With 45 minutes to go, I had to pack up my shit and gun my way across Birmingham to my mother-in-law's house, as if I was in *Grand Theft Auto*. 'Get out of my way, you prats. Goldbridge has a football show to present.' When I arrived, I quickly ushered my bewildered mother-in-law into her bedroom to watch *Strictly* and then broadcast my first talkSPORT show from her living room. We got the job done, but I'm telling you, Virgin almost had blood on their hands.

Since that debacle, the show has gone from strength to strength. I love doing it and interacting with other fans, setting the world to rights. Now I've got a taste for it and I fancy doing some more in the future. I was well up for getting involved when Laura Woods left the breakfast show. Jim White even told me I'd be good at it, but I never got the call. Not yet, anyway. Hopefully, one day.

It feels like we've gone off on one big tangent here. Like Michael Aspel has arrived with a big red book while I've been working and said, 'Mark Goldbridge, this is your wanky life.' But listen, it's my book, so you'll just have to swivel on it. I think the whole point was: if you're getting fucked off with the game, you can set up a fan channel or something. Either way, if you do, try to do something original. There are enough fanboys out there already mugging Goldbridge off. They're like tribute acts, like Stars in Their Bloody Eyes.

'Tonight, Matthew, I'm going to be Mark Goldbridge.'

I think we can all agree there's only enough room in the world for one Goldbridge, and you're stuck with me, I'm afraid.


## WHEN FANS FIGHT BACK

'I'm as mad as hell, and I'm not gonna take this anymore.'

It's a bloody good line, this. It really is. Those movie aficionados among you will know it is passionately delivered by Peter Finch, dismayed at the decaying state of the world, in his Oscar-winning role in 1976's *Network*. The equivalent in the football world would be Neil Warnock shouting, 'It's a load of bollocks, that is.' Either way, both sentiments were well and truly felt by most football fans when the Super League was proposed in 2021.

Even now, this blows my mind. Who thought this was a good idea? It was the equivalent of giving a hand job to a corpse. Absolutely disgraceful and bloody pointless. I mean, all you're doing is embarrassing yourself. Unless you get a kick out of it. In which case, seek help. But it really was like the billionaire owners of football clubs all got together and thought: *Everyone already thinks we're a right bunch of pricks; let's prove them right, shall we?* It's not as if enough people think the likes of the Glazers and Daniel Levy are shameless prats as it is. In case you've forgotten just how bloody ridiculous this concept was, let me take you back.

Without any fan consultation whatsoever, the billionaire owners of the world's biggest football clubs decided to set up their own league and lock everyone else out. They might as well have called it The Prat League. The hall of shame included Manchester United, Manchester City, Chelsea, Liverpool, Spurs (what the bloody hell were they doing there?), Arsenal, Real Madrid, Barcelona, Atlético Madrid, Juventus, AC Milan and Inter Milan. Why share the spoils with a Crystal Palace or a Brentford, or risk missing out on the top four to Brighton, or even face relegation, when they could just fuck them off forever. There would be no more Premier League or Champions League either. Decades of history and tradition flushed down the toilet thanks to the greed of a few billionaires. I mean, how has this even got past the planning stage? What a load of bollocks. The idea has more holes in it than a hedgehog's pillow.

These bunch of cretins foolishly thought the fans of their clubs would accept the concept of a 'Super League'. Here's a shit sandwich, peasants; enjoy the peanuts. If a few were upset with this prospect, then fuck 'em. They reasoned they could afford to lose a few traditional fans in exchange for a new, young and prosperous worldwide audience. Talk about misreading the room. They also failed to grasp why we love football at the most basic level. For most of us, it's not just the prospect of glory. It's the rivalry, the competition, the jeopardy of missing out or even the threat of relegation. For Manchester United, in particular, it's triumph over adversity. Where's the adversity in a Super League?

As I said before, one of the main reasons I became a Manchester United fan was because I connected with the club's story. From the tragedy of Munich, where the Busby Babes were all but wiped out, the club had somehow risen from the ashes to win the European Cup a decade later. This was forever planted into the Manchester United DNA. This was why so many of us loved our club. If you took this away, then our club would become unrecognisable. It was just a brand name stuck on a lifeless zombie. All our reasons for supporting it would disappear. And now the Glazers were happily going along with abolishing the European Cup, the competition that had come to define our club. I mean, what the actual fuck did they think they were doing?

Almost immediately, puff PR statements from the clubs flooded the media. Like John Terry in his full kit, they tried pulling the wool over everyone's eyes. They must have thought we were all stupid. I instantly knew this was nothing more than a shameless power grab for a few billionaires to make more money for them and their hedge funds. They didn't give a toss about the game. Most of them didn't even understand what made it so special in the first place. They didn't go to stadiums when they were kids, in all weathers, watching a shit team try to defy the odds. They'd never played on shitty park pitches in the pissing rain, getting covered in dog shit. The only reason they had got involved in football in the first place was to add even more millions to their bank account. As far as I was concerned, if the Super League went ahead, then football could swivel on it. It was as good as dead. You could shove it right up your arse. However, I feared we had already lost the fight. These talks had clearly been going on for months. TV deals had already been agreed upon, and the billionaire owners had laid much of the PR groundwork. Sneaky little pricks that they are.

Thankfully, most fans weren't having this nonsense. We know a shit idea when we see one. We weren't having 'The 39th Game', and we weren't having this. Stick that right in the bin where it belongs. For once, all of football was united to fight for the survival of our game. United, Liverpool, City, and fans from all over came together. It was like The Avengers against a bunch of twats. I had never been prouder to be a football fan. This was above any rivalry. Apart from a few idiots who just wanted to see their club dominate, no matter the cost, the vast majority were united as one against it.

The backlash from social media and the physical protests soon saw those behind the Super League recede faster than Pep's hairline. Within days of its announcement, the Super League had been crushed. However, there was still plenty of talk that it wasn't completely dead. And when the Glazers are involved, United fans know not to trust a word. As anger against the proposals continued to grow, social media brought United fans together to blockade Old Trafford before the game with Liverpool. With the Liverpool team bus unable to reach the stadium, the game was called off.

Football fans had united and had claimed victory over the billionaires and their hedge funds. It proved that we were not powerless. That we do, in fact, still control the game. Stick that in your pipe and smoke it. The Glazers, Dan Levy, Sheikh Mansour, John Henry and all the rest of you prats, your boys took a hell of a beating!

But this is far from the only incident over the years where the fans have been presented with an idea and said, 'Oh fuck off. Is the circus in town?' In 2012, Cardiff City owner Vincent Tan promised to bankroll the club as long as it changed its blue shirts to red. That's not going to fly, is it? The club had played in blue since 1908. The club's nickname was the Bluebirds, for fuck's sake. But because a billionaire owner's lucky colour was red, he thought he had good reason to change it. What the fucking hell was he drinking in Malaysia? It sure as hell wasn't delicious Diet Coke. You really can't blame Cardiff fans for losing their shit. Some fans walked away, others protested. Some geniuses even wrote to Malaysian media companies to shame Tan into leaving. He tried to hold firm for a while, but eventually, with dwindling attendances and pressure from supporter groups, he announced that the club would be reverting to blue. What a bloody waste of time. These people might have a load of money, but honestly, when it comes to football, they couldn't pour water out of a jug if it had the instructions on the bottom.

In the 1980s, a change in colour was the least of Reading's and Oxford's fans' worries. In 1982 millionaire newspaper bellend Robert Maxwell bought Oxford United. Alarm bells should really be ringing already. This just isn't going to end well, is it? Almost immediately, he did something bonkers, which, for Maxwell, is really saying something. He announced that he had agreed to merge Oxford with its hated rivals Reading. The new club would be known as the Thames Valley Royals and play at a new stadium. You're having a laugh, aren't you? To piss off your own fans is par for the course, but to do it to two clubs and to unite hated rivals in the process is a special kind of magic. Not even Paul Daniels and the lovely Debbie McGee could match this.

Maxwell told fans that 'nothing short of the end of the earth' would stop the merger, not even when Oxford fans held a 2,000-person sit-in at their ground and Reading fans organised a series of protest marches. Despite his big ideas and millions,

Maxwell was out of his depth, like a Hobbit wearing Timberlands in the deep end of a swimming pool. Reading fans pored through the legals and took Maxwell to court. There, they successfully challenged the transfer of shares, leaving Maxwell unable to take control and stopping the merger dead. All of that fuss, and money, just to look like a right wally.

All of this just goes to show we fans still have the power to protect our game. No matter how much money or big ideas some of these prats might have, they're nothing without us. Sure, some fancy pants knobhead will come up with another shit idea soon enough. Chelsea's Todd Boehly is gagging to come up with something. But when these prats do, they'll be met with more resistance than a Vinnie Jones reducer.

# 6

# PRIME CARLTON PALMER

There comes a time in every football fan's life when they have to admit something very painful; they're a shit footballer. They're just not going to make it as a pro. There's more chance of my nan climbing Mount Everest, and she's dead.

For some, the realisation comes early. Two left feet and a head like a 50-pence piece are no great indicators of future sporting success, although that didn't stop Harry Maguire. They're probably the lucky ones. They can immediately give up on any sporting dreams and just enjoy being a fan. Then there's the rest of us, clinging on, more in hope than any reason, like Steve McClaren and his brolly in the rain. Some of us might actually be pretty decent. There might even be trials for professional clubs along the way. You believe you've got what it takes. You're different.

Looking back, my belief that I was going to make it as a pro was a bit strange. I didn't actually play regularly for any team until I was around 14. The weird thing is, I still seemed to be playing all the time, whether with mates in the park, at break time or even in the back garden by myself. The main reason I didn't play Saturday league football was my parents were divorced, and that was when I would see my dad. I also didn't put myself forward for the secondary school team for the simple reason that I thought some of the players were bellends. There was no real evidence of this, but I just had a feeling, sort of like how you should keep Phil Jones away from corners. Besides, I was still very shy and far happier in my own company. However, when I was 14, some of my mates said I should at least go along to training. I was torn, but I could see they really enjoyed it, and I loved football. It seemed stupid not to at least give it a go. Well, fuck me, it was like tasting cheesecake for the first time. Wary at first, something not feeling quite right, but after just five minutes I loved it. Not only did I enjoy the football but I even realised that the bellends were actually alright. Some even became good friends.

In the early days I played as a left winger and fancied myself as Lee Sharpe. For some reason, I always preferred Sharpe to Giggs, mainly because he was a bit cooler and had an edge to him. I suppose I could play a bit. I was relatively quick and skilful and could hold my own physically, as by the age of 15, I was 6ft. I also like to think I could read the game well, so as time went on, I ended up playing centre back. That didn't mean I was a shit winger, alright. That's just what you can do when you're an all-rounder. I relished the physical challenge and fancied myself as a Franco Baresi, bringing the ball elegantly and calmly out of defence to set off attacks. Boy, you should have seen Goldbridge in his prime. There were skills to pay the bills and then some.

Listen, I can't have been that bad, as when I was 15, I was invited for a trial with Northampton Town, so swivel on that. Alright, alright, I know! We've all had trials! Just let me have my moment. I'm in my forties now, and this shit is all I've got left. I was actually playing really well until I got hit in the balls when trying to block a shot. You absolute fucking twat! It bloody stung, that. Y'know, when it feels like you might actually puke up a bollock? There were all these tough kids there as well, so I had to pretend like it didn't hurt. I had to go full Terry Butcher, playing through the pain like an English lion-heart. Even today, I look back and think, if I hadn't been hit in the balls, I might have ended up playing for Northampton Town. I could have been a Cobblers' legend. Maybe they'd even name a stand after me. Your loss, I'm afraid. And while Northampton didn't snap me up, I was convinced that my time would come again. This time when I had two working bollocks.

My school team was pretty decent and always in contention for trophies. One year, we beat our local rivals, Ratcliffe, in the cup final. It was great. Two busloads came to watch us play. It felt like being a big-time footballer. But the biggest prize of all came in the cup the following year. That year the final was to be played at Meadow Lane. An actual professional football stadium. Dreams didn't get any bigger than that, let me tell you. Go and play with your Lego, son; this has Goldbridge's name all over it.

We were determined to get there and pulverised most teams on our way to the semi-final. Then, typically, we faced a really tough team from Nottingham. Still, I fancied our chances. Better still, I knew there would be scouts at the game. This was my big chance. I was determined to take it. No bruised bollock was going to stop me this time.

I started the game at centre back and felt comfortable. A bit like Vidić and Ferdinand all rolled into one. Sure, they were a good team, but we were better. I was already imagining fending off scouts after the game. I might not even make it to Meadow Lane at this rate. I'd probably be tied down to a two-year YTS contract. Stuff your cup final. The big time was waiting. Then, disaster struck. The game boiled over and, in quick succession, we had two players sent off. Bloody hell! The odds might have been against us, but this only made me raise my game, like Roy Keane against Juventus in '99. I pushed into centre midfield and had a burst of energy like I'd never had before. It was as if I had necked a packet of Sherbet Dip and washed it down with a can of Monster. I was in more positions than a porn star with a bad knee. Despite being two men down and the game being frantic, it felt like it was in slow motion. That I had all the time in the world to do exactly as I wanted. Like a dad playing with a balloon against their kids. To be fair, it wasn't just me who was having a blinder. All of us dug in and played well beyond ourselves. We even managed to reach extra time. But finally, we broke, losing the game by one goal.

Talk about a kick in the balls, although this time, this was more metaphorical than physical. Whichever way I was kicked in the balls, I was still gutted. It seemed it had all been for bloody nothing. There would be no Meadow Lane, after all. Despite this, I thought that my performance might at least have caught the eye of a scout. I had just put on a masterclass.

As I forlornly walked towards the changing rooms, I saw a man in a big Adidas overcoat approach me. And no, he wasn't a paedo about to flash me. I feel like every time I say something, I need to stop and clarify it. Bloody nuisance, you lot. You can't say anything anymore without someone thinking of smut. Anyway, I'd never seen him before, but he just had that football scout look. Solid, grizzled, been around the block. I scanned his jacket for a club badge but saw nothing. Maybe he was with County, or Forest or maybe even Villa. Either way, this was it. 'Tonight, Matthew, I'm going to be a Premier League footballer.'

I slowed my stride as the man sidled up next to me, smelling of tobacco, Bovril and Deep Heat. I thought of what cool response I could nonchalantly come out with when he invited me to a trial. Something cocky like, 'Yeah, I'll have to check 'cos I've already been approached by Leeds.' Then, he opened his mouth. This was it. 'You were like prime Carlton Palmer out there,' he said, patting me on the back. Then he walked off and got into his car. 'Is that fucking it?' I thought. 'Prime fucking Carlton Palmer! Where's my fucking trial?' At that, the man sped out of the car park without giving me a second look. Fucking hell!

Let's be honest: prime Carlton Palmer wasn't so bad. Even if he did become a figure of fun, he still played for Leeds and England. However, out of all the great central midfielders playing in the league at the time, it pissed me off that this was the comparison that was made after the greatest game of my life. Yet there was no getting away from it. At 15 years old, I finally realised there would be no last-minute winners in front of the Stretford End. I was all washed up. A career as a professional footballer was not for me. I was devastated. Even then, I still told the school's career officer I was going to be a footballer.

'Be realistic, Mark. You've got no chance of that happening.'

'Who are you to stamp on my dreams! I'll bloody show you!'

Yeah, this isn't one of those stories. Fair play, they were right. I was so convinced I would make it that I didn't even apply to do my A Levels. Bloody idiot. Soon after, I discovered drink, rock 'n' roll and Oasis. Then began the dream of becoming the next Liam Gallagher. I couldn't sing or play a musical instrument, but I could grow cracking sideburns. Still, it's the dreams that keep us going sometimes.

I wasn't the only idiot out there to think like this. For most fans, this is the pedestal we put footballers on. For some reason, we see them as mythical beings, not real people. We dream to join them, to be one of them, to score last-minute winners for the team we love and to have the crowd chanting our name. 'One Mark Goldbridge! There's only one Mark Goldbridge!' While we can't all be pros, that doesn't mean the dream is over. There are still plenty of ways we can enjoy the good stuff without having to endure an Antonio Conte pre-season session. In fact, who needs to actually play football when you can just do all of this?

## THE SHARPIE SHUFFLE

The first goal celebration routine I vividly remember is Cameroon striker Roger Milla's from the 1990 World Cup. After every goal, he'd race to the corner flag, raise one hand in the air and wiggle his hips, almost like he was shagging it. Absolute magic. I loved it! Still lost to England, though, didn't they? But the player that really got me into goal celebrations was Lee Sharpe. He was our Picasso.

179

When United played Villa in 1993, Sharpe was on fire, scoring two great goals. But it was his goal celebrations that really caught my eye. This was the night the iconic Sharpie Shuffle was born. Racing to the corner flag, he placed his right hand on his left shoulder, the left hand on his right, then one hand on one hip, swiftly joined by the other hand on the opposite hip. Thrusting his groin suggestively forward, he raised his right hand to his lips, ran his fingers across them, and then flicked them towards the sky. What the fuck have I just seen? I was in awe. I hadn't seen moves like this since my Uncle Frank tried it on with the bridesmaids at a wedding that summer. Auntie Carol wasn't that impressed, mind, being as it was their wedding. But this was the absolute bollocks from Sharpey. It really didn't get much cooler than this. For weeks after I'd replicate the celebration every break time in the play-ground after banging a tennis ball into a doorway. For those teachers who had never seen the Sharpie Shuffle before, they must have thought my groin thrusts were a bit suspect, as there were a few looks of disapproval.

Sharpe didn't stop there. Great artists are never satisfied. Some players have one memorable celebration in their locker. Old Lee Sharpe was just getting started. Next came the Elvis celebration, racing to the corner flag, pulling it back, shaking his hips and then singing into it like a microphone. It was infectious. We all loved Sharpe's celebrations, everyone except Sir Alex, that is. Bloody spoilsport. Sharpe admitted as much while a guest on the *Undr the Cosh* podcast. In 1993, after Sharpe had scored the winner at Goodison Park in a 1–0 win over Everton, he performed the Sharpie Shuffle in celebration. Good times all round. However, when he got on the team bus, buzzing at his goal and the three points, Sir Alex couldn't give less of a fuck: 'He's stomping up the bus,' Sharpe revealed, 'comes straight up to me, right in my face and says, "What was all that fucking carry on after you scored, you little fucking shit. Fucking get your feet on the floor; who do you think you are? Fucking stop that." And I'm like sliding down my seat.'

The Sharpe celebration era was at an end, to be replaced by Alan Shearer's one-hand salute. Boring! Thankfully, there have still been plenty of celebrations to enjoy over the years: the Klinsmann dive, Ravanelli putting his shirt over his head, Bebeto rocking the baby, Gazza's dentist chair, Kazenga LuaLua's double somersault, Peter Crouch's robot and Jimmy Bullard's 'team talk'. I also used to love ex-Fulham striker Facundo Sava hiding a superhero mask around the pitch or in his shin pad, ready to whip it out as soon as he had scored a goal.

One impromptu celebration that also blew my mind was when Sylvain Wiltord scored against United at Old Trafford in 2002 to win the title for Arsenal. As he was celebrating, Kanu suddenly did a star jump over his head. He wasn't even leaning down. Kanu actually jumped over a grown man while he was standing up. It's ridiculous. Far more impressive than anything he ever did on the football pitch. (Alright, Arsenal fans. Don't take the bait. It's easy. Just smile, shake your head at that naughty boy Goldbridge, at it again, then move on. You don't have to go all AFTV on me. It's just another Goldbridge dub.)

Celebrations are meant to be a bit of fun, but some have led to players getting an absolute bollocking. When Emmanuel Adebayor scored for Manchester City against his former club, Arsenal, he raced towards their fans to celebrate in front of them like a demented ferret. For this, he earned himself a £25,000 fine. Come on. Give over. Their fans were giving him stick, so why should he be punished for celebrating in front of them? Don't give it out if you can't take it back.

As much as I admire Lee Sharpe's dedication to his craft, no doubt practising thrusting his hips for hours in his hotel room mirror, it's not my all-time favourite. Most of us can pull off the Sharpie Shuffle. It's like the Macarena of football celebrations. It's just a bit of good fun and shows you don't take yourself too seriously. But some celebrations are reserved for the finest footballers in the land. For anyone to even think of emulating them would look very, very silly. I'm talking specifically about Eric Cantona's celebration against Sunderland at Old Trafford in 1996.

First of all, the goal preceding it was a masterpiece. They could hang it in a museum. After picking up the ball on the halfway line, Cantona brilliantly turned two players, then played a one-two with Brian McClair on the edge of the box. Shaping up as if he was going to give it a good twat, he suddenly lofted his right foot under the ball. Everything seemed to stand still for a moment as it sailed through the air, over the stranded Sunderland keeper, then delicately dropped into the top corner. It was a moment of genius. Most players might have lost their heads. Not our Eric. Without so much as cracking a smile, he puffed out his chest like a gladiator in the Colosseum and turned to take in his adoring fans. 'Have some of that, ya pricks!' It was almost an affront to him that there was a sense of amazement about the goal. Only a great player like Cantona could get away with it.

Now, while I'm all for players celebrating, I draw the line at fan routines in the stands. I'm talking specifically about Manchester City's 'The Poznan'. This is the shittest celebration out there. People putting their arms around each other, turning around and bouncing up and down? Do me a favour. You've got to reassess your life if you're getting involved in this nonsense.

Anyway, now I've got my pop at City out of the way, remember, celebrations make the game fun. Embrace them. Copy them when you play five-a-side with your mates. Feel like a kid again. What's the point of twatting a ball in the top corner if you won't celebrate properly afterwards? And if a routine is too much bother for you, then you can just do what Italy's Marco Tardelli did after scoring in the 1982 World Cup final: go absolutely mental. But this might be more appropriate for a World Cup final than a kickaround with your kids.

## FULL KIT WANKER

In art classes at school, my mate and I used to spend hours designing football kits. It wasn't part of the lesson, it's just what we wanted to do. I'm a rebel like that. Stuff painting a flowerpot. I'd draw a neon technicolour United kit instead. Have some of that! But doing this wasn't enough.

So convinced was I of my artistic genius that after I was done, I'd find the address for Umbro and send my designs off. For some reason, I never heard back. No wonder Umbro had to be bought out by Nike in the end. You missed a trick there, lads. My United designs could have kept you afloat.

For most of us, wearing a kit as a kid wasn't just to show the world the team we supported. It was more than that. It was like Superman putting his costume on. Once we had that kit on, we could imagine how it felt to be a pro footballer. Suddenly, we were one of our heroes. Anything felt possible.

Growing up, I was obsessed with football kits. Obviously, I had a fair few United ones. It was a real golden era for kit design as well. My favourite was probably the United away kit from the 1992/3 season. It was mint: royal blue, with black paint splattered on it, an oversized club badge in the print and the iconic Sharp sponsor across the front. A stone-cold classic. I didn't bloody have it, though, did I? When I went to buy it, they'd sold out of all the shirts in my size. I couldn't believe it. I still bought the shorts, though. I loved them so much I would wear the blue away shorts with the red home shirt. I didn't care how ridiculous I looked.

This was far from the only great United shirt in the nineties. I also loved the black away strip from the 1993/4 season, with Sharp Viewcam as the sponsor. It's the one Cantona wore when he kung-fu kicked the Palace fan in the stands at Selhurst Park. I loved that kit. I remember going into town on a Saturday morning and buying it. I was like an Andrex puppy with a packet of bog roll. There was also the away shirt from the 2001/2 season that was reversible. I'm sure this is the only kit in Premier League history that did this. It was gold on one side and white on the other. I've still got it somewhere. You'll know when I've had a chance to clean out my attic as I'll suddenly be wearing it one day.

Despite this, my favourite United home shirt is unsurprisingly the 1999 treble-winning number. I got it for Christmas that year, with the number 7 and my name on the back. I absolutely loved it and wore it all the time. When I moved out, I left it at home and it eventually found its way into the loft with all of my other childhood things. One year, I went up there and found everything had gone! Some fucker had sold my *He-Man*, *A-Team* and *Star Wars* toys. Castle Grayskull and Snake Mountain were goners. Even Mr. T didn't survive. My whole childhood had been binned by some heartless bastard. They'd all probably be worth a few quid or two today and all. For a few weeks I was like Columbo, trying to catch the culprit. No one owned up to it.

However, while all my toys had been binned, my football shirts seemed to have survived the cull. This was something, I suppose. At least the prat had some sort of conscience, or so I thought. While my treasured United top from 1999 was still there, it had black tar all over it. My brother had worn it while tarmacking the fucking roads! I was livid. It was my most cherished shirt, and now it was ruined.

It wasn't just United kits I loved, though. My mate had a cracking Blackburn away kit, which was black with red stripes. I liked it so much that I actually borrowed it and never gave it back. The England kits from Italia 90 were also belters, but I never got one at the time. Finally, a few years back, I was doing a photo shoot with a certain betting company, and they made me wear the red away kit from 1990. *I'm having that*, I thought. It's still in my wardrobe, kept as far away from my brother and tarmac as possible. It took me over 30 years, but I got it in the end.

In the mid-1990s, I even had a green Germany away kit.

Don't start. It was reduced in the Freemans catalogue, so my mum got it for me. While Germany haunted my dreams after Italia 90 and Euro 96, I still thought it was a great kit and was more than happy to wear it. Not everyone was so open-minded though. I remember wearing it in the Co-op, and a grown man booed me. A bloody grown man booing a kid. I suppose he had a point though. So, if you are going to wear a kit out and about, it might be best to take into account your surroundings before you commit a hate crime.

To become a Full Kit Wanker though it's all about the extras. I used to love wearing my favourite player's boots as well. PUMA Kings were always my favourite. I loved the big white tongue that used to flap over the laces. I'd polish and dubbin up the black leather for hours. I don't suppose kids do that anymore, as all the boots are synthetic. I loved the smell. Some kids sniffed glue, I sniffed dubbin. I don't think that counted as a Class A . . . Dubbin's where it's at, lads, and it won't get you in any bother, either. Saying that, I'd better check the facts before I start a dubbin-sniffing epidemic.

Despite loving them, I had a bit of a disaster with the first pair of Kings I bought. After wearing them in a game, I realised nearly all the studs had fallen out. I didn't know you had to tighten them. Why aren't there instructions for things like this? Kids are stupid. Clearly, the designers had never had children. At least tightening studs is another thing you don't have to worry about today, as everyone pretty much wears blades.

When I was earning big money on my paper round I remember splashing out on a pair of Reebok Astroturf boots because Ryan Giggs wore them. I swear they were magic, like the ones Jimmy Grimble wore. Some of the goals I scored in them would break the internet today. I felt like I could do anything. No wonder Giggs was so bloody good wearing them. It was like a cheat code.

I also loved Adidas Predators. I remember seeing them for the first time on *Blue Peter*. The ex-Liverpool player Craig Johnston was on the programme showing off this insane new boot he'd designed. He'd placed big rubber ridges on the front of the boot, which he claimed could make you kick the ball harder and add more swerve. I was sold. I had to have them, even if they cost £120, which was an absolute fortune back then. My stepdad got me a pair for Christmas, and I genuinely thought they worked. I swear. I could absolutely twat a ball in a pair of those. However, while Predators are still around, they no longer have the rubber ridges at the front. Is that an admission from Adidas that the concept was basically a load of crap? Whatever. I still thought I was chocolate.

As well as shirts and boots, I also loved checking out all the quirky little habits footballers had so I could copy them. There'd be John Barnes wearing ladies' stockings or Thierry Henry with his socks pulled over his knees to keep his legs warm. Then there was Patrick Vieira smearing the front of his shirt with a big blob of Vicks VapoRub or Robbie Fowler wearing a nose strip. These last two tricks were apparently to help with breathing. I think they did fuck all, but that didn't stop me from copying them. These days, there's Jack Grealish with his tight shorts and tiny shin pads. Apparently, these are actually children's pads, which he started wearing when he was 15 and thought brought him luck. I just thought they were an homage to Leicester City legend Steve Claridge.

Sadly, as age creeps up on us, we no longer get to wear fancy technicolour boots. We'd look weird smearing Vicks over our work shirts, and the days of wearing a full replica kit to look like our heroes are over. However, if it makes you feel good, then you do you, hun. There are still other choices, though. You don't have to go Full Kit Wanker in the latest home strip. Instead, buy yourself a replica shirt of one you used to wear as a kid. These are often design classics and it can still look great wearing them casually or even to games. I also love wearing United's training gear. The hoodies, in particular, are magnificent. So, just because you might be knocking on a bit, don't feel like you can't rock a replica shirt and feel like Superman.

## BECOME A STYLE GOD

Being a fan isn't always about purchasing the latest replica kit or copying what players wear on the pitch. You can show your support in other ways that are not only far more cost-effective but fun. You can dress like your favourite player instead. No, I'm not talking about going as Harry Maguire for Halloween. You don't want to scare the kids. I mean, dressing like them when they're being normal. Not that they're not normal. Some of them definitely aren't, but that's a different kettle of fish altogether.

Granted, dressing like your favourite player has its pitfalls. Congratulations on your curly mullet if you chose Ipswich's Ian Marshall as your nineties style icon. There's also a reason Neville Southall titled his autobiography *The Binman Chronicles*. Big Nev might have been the best goalkeeper in the world in his prime, but he certainly wasn't known for his sartorial elegance. However, if you pick a player who is a genuine style icon, then you're going to have a lot of fun and compliments in and out of the stadium. Think of it as football fan fancy dress. Kids go to parties dressed as Batman. You go to football dressed like Dominic Calvert-Lewin, although that might make a great Halloween costume as well, come to think of it.

There's been a few so-called style icons in my time as a football fan. Like I said before, I was particularly partial to Chris Waddle's mullet. Thankfully, there are no polaroids lying around of little Mark with a short back and sides and a flowing mane. To be fair, mine was more Scott Robinson from

*Neighbours* than Chris Waddle. I still pulled it off, though, just about.

The first time I really remember wanting to dress like a footballer was during Gazzamania. (Don't laugh. When you hear this, I bet you did, too.) After Italia 90, Gazza was probably the most famous person in the country. He even had a number 2 hit with 'Fog on the Tyne'! If you've heard Gazza sing, you'll appreciate how remarkable this is. The B-side 'Geordie Boys' was also a banger. If you fancy watching Gazza dance, the video on YouTube is great as well. Go on. Bugger off. I'll see you in five minutes.

If Gazza can become a pop star, why not a fashion icon? His preference for shell suits quickly became the staple fashion choice for boys and girls. Even dads were wearing them with their stonewash jeans. You can bet your life I had one. With this outfit, I could pretend to be Gazza on and off the pitch. The fit and material looked cool and they were cosy as well. I thought I was a sex machine at the school disco, bopping away to 'The One and Only' by Chesney Hawkes. Sadly, all good things have to come to an end.

For some, fashion just moves on. We can't all wear boot-cut jeans forever, although I hear they're making a comeback. But trust Gazza to pick a fashion trend that was a danger to life. It turns out that shell suit material is highly flammable. Do you remember that scene in 1985's *Santa Claus: The*

*Movie* where Dudley Moore's elf makes all those wooden toy bikes, and they all fall apart after Christmas Day? There must be thousands of kids who had Gazza shell suits for Christmas in 1990, only to have their parents put them in the bin before the year was out. That'll teach us to copy Gazza's fashion sense. After all, this is a guy who took the team bus at Middlesbrough for a joy ride and crashed it. That certainly didn't stop us, though. By Euro 96, Gazza's bleached blond crop was all the rage. Some of us tried to copy it by putting Sun In in our hair and inadvertently went ginger. And if you're flicking to the photo section of this book to see the evidence, I've burned the lot. No one needs to see Goldbridge à la ginge.

For most of the nineties, Ryan Giggs, Lee Sharpe, Trevor Sinclair and Jamie Redknapp were your standard football style icons. Redknapp even had a range at Topman, but it was all very safe. I mean, this is the guy doing Skechers ads now. He's not going to rock the boat, is he? But by the mid-nineties, rather than a footballer, I wanted to look like Andre Agassi, and I was more than partial to fluorescent yellow cycling shorts. Looking back, I really did appreciate a good mullet.

When Britpop arrived in the middle of the decade, my whole world was turned upside down. Most of us suddenly wanted to dress, walk and talk like Liam Gallagher. Up and down the country, kids were all 'Mad Fer It' and walking like someone had just stuck a bottle up their bum. Shortly after Oasis appeared on *Top of the Pops*, there was a period when

I thought it was perfectly normal to wear sunglasses inside the local village pub. And I wasn't the only one. Yes, we were all drinking Red Stripe as well. Just think of that Kevin and Perry Oasis sketch and that was me after watching Knebworth, then and last year as it goes. Yet one footballer crossed over the football and music divide and embraced all of this, and then some.

Paul McGregor had come through the ranks at Forest, making a name for himself with a goal against Lyon in the UEFA Cup. Sporting a Beatles mop top, he looked cool as fuck. Then it turned out that being a professional footballer was just his side hustle. His main gig was as the lead singer for a band called Merc. As if training and starring for Forest on a Saturday afternoon wasn't enough, he'd also play gigs up and down the country. The media exposure only made Merc more popular. Soon, McGregor wasn't just featured in *Match* magazine but also the likes of *NME*. This all happened in a flash, but for a brief period of time, Paul McGregor was the coolest footballer in the country. I certainly thought so. Now, you could dress like a rock star and harbour dreams of being a professional footballer, all at the same time.

However, things for McGregor didn't quite work out on or off the football pitch. By 1999, he had been released by Forest. After a spell at Northampton Town, he retired at the age of 28. Merc didn't last much longer, either. Still, you can't have it fucking all, Paul. That's enough for two lifetimes.

Football fashion moved on quickly after McGregor left the scene. David Ginola and David James strutted their stuff in designer gear on catwalks in Milan. Liverpool famously turned up to the 1996 FA Cup final in cream Armani suits that made them all look like pints of jizz. I mean, seriously, whose fucking idea was that! Just a few years before, they'd been wearing shell suits. The foreign invasion then took it up a notch again. The Italian footballers arrived with tailored suits, chunky ties and fancy loafers. They might have looked cool, but it was all a bit high-end for most fans to copy. Even my paper round couldn't stretch to Armani suits, for fuck's sake.

Then, David Beckham arrived as our saviour. In a fashion whirlwind, we wore sarongs, blonde-tinted curtains, diamond earrings, Police sunglasses, shaved heads, braids and Alice bands. You name it, Beckham wore it, and so did we, even if some of us looked like Pat Butcher at a rave. That was the fun of the Beckham era. He looked cool as fuck, but it was also relatable. It was easy for fans to try and copy. Anyone could grab their sister's sarong, hair dye and diamond earrings and give it a go. Not that I did any of that . . . Anyway, let's move on.

Copying a player's style is all good, but believe it or not, they're often far from the coolest people in the stadium. Keep your hair on, Tom Davies. You lot might be paid millions and have access to the best stylists, but it's often the fans that are leading the style stakes. Terrace fashion has long been a thing. It all started in the seventies and eighties, when football fans followed their teams around Europe for the first time and came back with the latest clobber from the Continent. Adidas tracksuits and trainers in the eighties were particularly popular, especially on Merseyside, with Liverpool and Everton dominating Europe and going on lots of away trips. Football fans were suddenly at the cutting edge of fashion. Known as 'Casuals', they sported brands like Lyle & Scott, Stone Island, Fila, Sergio Tacchini and Pringle and became synonymous with terrace culture. Going to a game almost became like a fashion parade, and still is for some. Many a time I've been at a game and spotted a fellow fan's jacket or trainers and thought, *They're ace! I'm having those!*

Sadly, as you age, you stop dressing like your favourite footballer and veer more towards dressing like a pundit. Most of us resemble Danny Murphy after a Next sale rather than David Beckham. Still, if you do want an affordable way to emulate a Premier League footballer, then instead of splashing out on an expensive washbag, just throw all your toiletries into a Tesco carrier bag and carry them around like Arsenal's Kieran Tierney.

## SOCIAL MEDIA

'Fucking hell! It's Steve Hodge!'

We were on the school bus and had spotted a real-life footballer out in the wild. Hysteria quickly spread. It was as if we had spotted Super Gran. We knew it was him because, on the side of the car, it read 'Steve Hodge – Sponsored by Bristol Street Motors'. Imagine the stars of today going around with stuff like that on their cars. Back then, the pros loved it. So did we. Everyone was waving out of the windows, trying to get a reaction. It was all we spoke about for days.

Seeing a player out in the real world is one of the great buzzes of being a fan. Whether it's getting an autograph or a selfie with your favourite players, there is something really special about meeting your heroes in the flesh, especially when you're a kid. At that age, you think players are superhuman. You see them on television, on social media, in magazines. Then, all of a sudden, they're in front of you, carrying a Gucci washbag, Beats by Dre around their neck, smelling like an explosion at an aftershave factory.

As a kid, I was always too shy to ask a player for an autograph. Give over! I hear you say. I swear, it's true. You might not believe it now, but I was very reserved. I never wanted to stand out in any way. The thought of speaking to a professional footballer would have terrified me. I once stood next to

Des Walker and I was scared shitless. It was like meeting the Honey Monster.

These days, it's harder than ever to see a player when you're out and about. You certainly won't see them when you're doing your Tesco shop. A lot of them are like Hollywood royalty. Surrounded by security guards in high-walled mansions, roped off in VIP private rooms. It's difficult to get anywhere near them. There's also the fact that many players find fan interactions awkward and avoid them at all costs. Sometimes, you have to remember that these are usually young kids in their twenties whose sole talent in life is being able to kick a ball better than most people. Some are not comfortable with all of the attention. No wonder they sign a scrap of paper or pose for a selfie without barely making eye contact or uttering a word. Why do you think most players look scared in selfies they have with fans? Very few smile or look happy with the situation. Look into their eyes. They can't wait to get away. They share the same haunted look Aaron Lennon had when he signed for Everton in 2015.

Why go to all that effort anyway? Rather than have to track a player down and have a two-second awkward encounter, just find them on social media. Most players are on there. Say hello. Respond to a post. Send them a joke. A response from a player on social media to one of your replies is surely just as cool as any autograph or selfie. This does, however, come with its own issues.

A lot of players have social media managers working for them these days. Often, the post you see hasn't even been written by the player. Maybe it hasn't even been seen by the player. Some players have social media just to build their 'brand'. That's why most of what they say is so bloody moronic. 'We go again.' 'Special thanks to the fans . . .' Safe, boring, no chance of causing offence. It's not hard to tell when a social media manager is providing all of the content. Sometimes, though, the players have inadvertently outed themselves, and look like right prats.

In 2021 Spurs took on Croatia's Dinamo Zagreb in the Europa League. After winning the first leg at home 2–0, they expected to cruise into the quarter-finals. But then again, this is Spurs. Only God and José Mourinho know how, but they ended up losing the second leg 3–0 and crashed out of Europe. Joe Hart's media team clearly didn't get the memo. At the final whistle, they posted 'JOB DONE' on Hart's Instagram page and a screenshot of the 3–0 loss, thinking it had been a win. Talk about a clusterfuck. This isn't an Arsène Wenger winter coat. It shouldn't be that difficult. Understandably, Spurs fans were not amused at their goalkeeper's apparent delight at crashing out of Europe. In full panic mode, Hart wasted little time throwing his social media manager under the bus and in the bin. If you can't get a result right, then there's no hope for you, really, is there? But Hart is far from the only player to look like a right berk on social media.

In 2016, following a 1–0 defeat to West Ham, Sunderland striker Victor Anichebe sent the following instruction to his social media manager: 'Can you tweet something like . . . Unbelievable support yesterday and great effort by the lads! Hard result to take! But we go again!' Anichebe had, of course, only meant for the second part of the message to be seen by the public. This was too much work for his social media guy, who posted the whole message instead. Shambles. A total and utter fucking shambles. You've also got to ask, what the fuck is Victor Anichebe doing with a social media manager? What a fucking gig! 'Sat on the bench again. Scored no goals. Off to Tesco.' I mean, what type of brand are we building here? Unbelievable.

To be fair to some of these players, posting on social media is obviously far too difficult for them to wrap their heads around. Let's just consider this absolute gem from Wayne Rooney in 2011: 'Hi rio do u want picking up in the morning pal.' Rooney had obviously meant to send this to Rio Ferdinand via text. But instead, he somehow found his way onto his Twitter account, like a drunk searching for the light switch to have a piss, and posted it for the world to see. How do you not twig that you're not sending a text? Bloody basics, Wayne. Still, out of all the things Rooney might have publicly sent, maybe it wasn't so bad. In his early experimentations on social media, Rooney got involved in a spat with a fan, which saw him post, 'I'll put u asleep within 10 seconds, little girl. Don't say stuff and not follow up on it. I'll be waiting.' Unsurprisingly, Wayne has been a lot quieter on social media in recent years.

Again, Rooney is far from the only player who finds social media difficult. Following Aston Villa losing 6–0 to Liverpool in 2016, Villa defender Joleon Lescott posted a photograph of an expensive Mercedes after the game. Yeah, that's one way to win over the fans, Joleon. Panicking like a cat trying to bury their shit in a marble floor, he claimed he had posted the photo by accident after sitting on his phone while driving. I'm reaching for my Jimmy Hill chin and stroking it vigorously. This smells awfully like the dog ate my homework. Unsurprisingly, Villa fans weren't amused and Lescott barely played for the club again.

Even when players are writing their posts themselves, it can often end up as a total clusterfuck. In 2017 French striker Antoine Griezmann simply posted: 'I miss her.' All very cryptic. So of course Paul Pogba comes wading in with the funnies: 'bet she bad.' Wink wink. Smiley face. Lads! Lads! Yeah, except she wasn't, though, Paul, as Griezmann made clear with his response: 'my grandma, bro.' Seriously, Paul. Go dye your hair or something. Leave the funnies to Goldbridge.

Some posts can't be blamed on misunderstandings or even an accident. Some are just sheer, mind-blowing stupidity. In 2018 Samir Nasri posed for a photograph after receiving treatment at a therapy clinic called Drip Doctors, which was then posted on social media. WADA thought this all looked a bit dodgy, so they launched an investigation. It turns out it was very fucking dodgy, and Nasri received an 18-month playing ban. Talk about shitting your own bed.

Now, I haven't painted a pretty picture of footballers and social media so far, but player and fan interaction online can be a lot of fun. I especially like it when they're prepared to give it back if a fan has a go at them. I have some experience of this. Once upon a time, I expressed my opinion that David de Gea was a better goalkeeper than Thibaut Courtois. Alright, things have gone south for Dave since, but this was a perfectly valid view at the time. But Courtois certainly didn't think so. He started by posting three Champions League emojis under my post, then went to town. What made this exchange even better was that at the time Courtois was in the news after proposing to his supermodel girlfriend. You've got to laugh. A multimillionaire Champions League winner, on a yacht with a supermodel, and he's saying: 'Hold on, love, I've just got to take that prick Goldbridge down a peg or two.'

Either way, me and old Thibaut withdrew our swords and shared our opinions like gentlemen of the country manor. I enjoyed the exchange, and it really warms my heart to see a good social media conversation between a player and a fan. However, this doesn't always go so well.

Scott McTominay and Fred clearly weren't too happy when I expressed my opinion that they were one of the worst centre midfield pairings in the Premier League. I also don't suppose they were too chuffed when I affectionally coined the phrase 'McFred', which went viral and became their accepted name whenever they appeared on the same team sheet. Now, I hold my hands up. I wasn't particularly complimentary about their ability as a duo. At the time, there wasn't an awful lot to be complimentary about. I wasn't abusive, though. I was just expressing my opinion, no matter how right or wrong I might be, that they were shit. Turns out McFred thought I was very wrong. Like a nineties WWF tag team, both players proceeded to block me. That's their right, but I thought it was a shame. I'd have much preferred them to come back at me or any fan who might be having a pop. Show me I'm wrong. Explain why I'm a big-mouth prat who knows nothing about football. I'm a big boy. Destroy me with hard facts. Maybe they tried to answer me with their performances on the football pitch. If so, it wasn't a success.

While I think it's healthy for fans and players to converse on social media and share opinions, there's also a darker side to this. The racist abuse some players get is disgusting. After their penalty misses in the Euro 2020 final, Marcus Rashford, Jadon Sancho and Bukayo Saka received some vile messages. There is no place for this in football or society. I despair when I see this. I really do. If you're racist and can't keep your mouth shut, then go and play with your Lego or something. Not that it makes you racist if you do play with Lego. Each to their own, but just don't be a bloody prat. Wise up. Educate yourself. Either way, there's no place in society for it.

Like I said, I'd urge fans and players to interact more on social media. It would be great to bridge the gap between each other. The players can understand where the fans are coming from. Meanwhile, the fans get to speak to their heroes. Go ahead. Make each other's day. Hug it out like Robbie Williams and Gary Barlow.

# 7

# SAVING FOOTBALL

Learning how to survive football as a fan is all well and good. But as Meghan Markle once said in an impoverished African village, 'It's not enough to just survive . . . you've got to thrive.' So, let's take a quick time out and look at ways we can improve the game.

In my time following football, numerous attempts have been made to change the game and how we consume it. Who can forget when the Premier League first came along, and Sky introduced Monday Night Football, with adverts promising a 'Whole New Ball Game'. I always remember Matt Le Tissier on a bench in the adverts doing keepy-uppies to the sound of 'Alive and Kicking'. Absolute magic and a lot harder to do than you think. It was soon clear that everything had indeed changed. Previously half-time entertainment had consisted of some bloke with a cigarette rolling the pitch. Suddenly, we had The Shamen performing their number one hit 'Ebeneezer

Goode', chanting, 'E's are good! E's are good!' while cheer-leaders danced around them. It was mental. Total lunacy. I loved it. Sadly, this didn't last long.

I hate change for the sake of it. Like, why does every team name a goalkeeper on the bench these days? This has ruined one of the great spectacles of the game. Previously, when a team's goalkeeper was sent off or injured, there was a good chance one of the outfield players had to go in goal. Seconds before, a world-class player would be in their comfort zone, and then they were in goal, looking like they'd never seen a ball before in their life. During a Europa League match against Greek side Asteras Tripolis, Spurs were down to ten men after Hugo Lloris was sent off. Harry Kane, who had scored a hat-trick, volunteered to go in goal in his place. He might be bloody good at putting goals in the net, but he's not much cop at keeping them out, let me tell you. He was like a newborn lamb trying to stop a pack of hungry wolves from eating the last Krispy Kreme doughnut. Yet, while we all had a good old laugh at Kane in goal, every now and again, one player has a blinder.

Vinnie Jones's moment came in 1995 when he had to go in goal for Wimbledon in a game at St James' Park after keeper Paul Heald was sent off. It was entertaining enough to see one of the game's infamous hotheads give it a crack between the sticks. However, what made it even better was he was really bloody good. After thwarting Les Ferdinand and David Ginola, he even had time to do some keepy-uppies. He might have conceded three goals, but that had more to do with his defenders being carved open like a Christmas turkey than anything Vinnie did.

Some changes have, however, made the game better. Take the back pass rule, for instance. You forget how boring football could be before that was brought in. For the last ten minutes of games, teams would constantly pass the ball back to their goalkeeper to waste time. Liverpool were notorious for this. Bruce Grobbelaar would roll the ball to Alan Hansen, who'd fuck around for a few seconds before passing the ball back. Grobbelaar would pick the ball up, bounce it a few times, look around, then throw it back to Hansen. On and on this would go, sucking the life out of a game. Imagine Mourinho or Conte teams if the back pass rule hadn't been brought in? There'd be no parking the bus. The ball would never leave the penalty area.

Thankfully, the back pass rule not only stopped time-wasting but revolutionised the game. Goalkeepers suddenly had to be good with their feet. The first few seasons after the rule was introduced in 1992 were hilarious. Keepers like Mark Bosnich, who were great with their hands, revealed they had two feet like flippers. Goalkeepers just weren't prepared for it. They were the weird kids in school who couldn't play football, so volunteered to go in goal. There was total panic at times. Rather than take any chances or try to play out from the back, they repeatedly thunderbastarded the ball out of play. Now, most Premier League teams base a lot of their tactics around their keepers being good with their feet. Ederson and Alisson are so good that they give outfield players a run for their money. But we've gone too far the other way. Some have forgotten that a keeper's primary purpose is to prevent goals from going in. It's all very well passing the ball out from the back, but if you have arms like baguettes, what use are you? Bring back De Gea!

In recent years, there have been a few attempts to change the game, mostly thanks to our American friends. It's insane to me that after buying a Premier League club because football is the most popular sport in the world, they then want to change the game to copy American sports leagues. We've seen attempts to set up a Super League, 'The 39th game' and even 'The Todd Boehly Cup final', basically a north vs south game. All are crap ideas and have so far been run out of town. While American billionaires think they know how to improve the game, no one ever asks the fans what we want. So, like Del Boy on his market stall, let me flog you a few of my ideas on how to revolutionise our game and have a bit of fun at the same time.

## LESS FOOTBALL

Sometimes more isn't better. We didn't need to see more Ole Gunnar Solskjaer as a manager. No one wants to see more

Michael Owen as a pundit. And there was only so much of Wout Weghorst us United fans could take. However, you might think that more football would be a good thing. You'd be wrong.

Despite footballers already playing too many games, and players' fitness being stretched to the max, some wally still thought that we should add more extra time on at the end of matches. Referees are now taking serious note of the time the ball has been out of play during each half, in an attempt to stop time-wasting. Now, we regularly see a minimum of five minutes added on at half-time and as much as ten minutes or longer at full-time. Games are regularly lasting more than 100 minutes.

If you add this up across three games a week, we are now asking players to play nearly another half of football across that time. It's unsustainable. At some point, you've got to think of player welfare. A recent PFA survey also found that 60 per cent of players were against this new rule, as they believe the extra workload is causing more injuries and making it harder to recover between games. A mid-season review also backed this up. It was found that there were 15 per cent more injuries at this point in 2023 than in the four previous seasons. It's not rocket science to say that the quality of the football goes down with more injured and fatigued players. I mean, bloody hell! They should have spoken to Goldbridge first. I could have put this idea in the bin as soon as it left their mouths. The demands on players are becoming ridiculous.

I'm sure we'd all like to be the lead singer in a rock band, but that doesn't mean you want to do a concert three times a day. Your throat would get a bit sore, for one thing.

I get why people want to stop time-wasting, but there's another way to stop it: bring in a stopwatch. Put a set time limit – say, 20 seconds – in place for things like throw-ins, free kicks and substitutions. If a player goes over the limit they either forfeit the throw-in or free kick or get carded. This would also stop ludicrous situations where players get carded for apparent 'time-wasting'. In a game against Crystal Palace in August 2023, Arsenal defender Takehiro Tomiyasu was booked for taking too long to take a throw-in. He had the ball in his hands for just 8 seconds. Eight bloody seconds! It's ridiculous. But no exact rule exists to say how long is too long for a player to take a throw-in. The decision is purely subjective. A time limit would get the game moving faster and prevent subjective decisions like this.

Rugby was facing similar issues to football and opted to put a time limit in place. Now, when there's a penalty, a player has 60 seconds to take the kick from the moment they decide to go for the posts. During the Rugby World Cup in 2023, England's Owen Farrell (it had to be bloody England) somehow fell foul of this and, after taking too long, had to forfeit taking the kick. Too bloody right as well. How long do you need to kick a ball between two posts? Get on with the game. Some of us have to get to bed.

# VAR

As much as I'd love to say they're a bunch of whining knob-heads, I actually feel sorry for Liverpool. There, you have it. Clip me up. This is what VAR has reduced me to.

Look at Luis Díaz's goal being wrongly disallowed for offside against Spurs in the 2023/4 season. I was fuming. Raging, in fact. Before VAR, there were, of course, still appalling decisions. But a referee or linesman had a split second to come to a conclusion – it's no wonder they got some things wrong. VAR was meant to stop this human error. That was the dream we were sold: *no more controversy*. What a load of bollocks that was. We now know it's somehow made things worse. Despite being able to watch multiple replays of incidents from lots of different angles, it's staggering how officials still can't make the right decisions. The disallowed Díaz goal was a masterpiece in clusterfucking the fuck out of a simple call. Standards are on the floor right now.

Listen, I get that some decisions are subjective. Whether a certain tackle is worthy of a red card can still be debated. Decisions like that can be analysed and debated to death, with everyone having divergent opinions. But offsides are different. You're either offside or you're not. We even have technology now that can call an offside if a player's toenail is in the wrong place. It was used in the World Cup and in the Champions

League to good effect, so how can the domestic league still get it so badly wrong? I'm sick and bloody tired of it.

Things aren't helped by ridiculous statements on the issue, such as by the likes of former referee Mike Dean. On the podcast *Up Front* in August 2023, Dean admitted that when working as the VAR in Tottenham's game against Chelsea the previous year, he turned a blind eye to Spurs defender Cristian Romero pulling Marc Cucurella's hair just before Tottenham scored a last-minute equaliser. Sounds a bit dodgy to me, Mike, but I'm sure you've got a good explanation. Except he hasn't. He admitted that he didn't alert referee Anthony Taylor to the foul before the goal because he didn't want his mate to suffer any more abuse from the managers or the crowd. You fucking what? It defies belief. If you don't laugh, you'll cry. This is the shit they're actually telling us with their own mouths! What's going on behind closed doors then? They're as useful as a musical instrument invented by Dion Dublin.

The fact that VAR still allows these fuck-ups proves it's not worth the hassle. What makes it even worse are the long breaks in play every bloody time VAR is used. Some of them can take as long as five minutes. The officials in the VAR room are slower than a snail's funeral at getting simple decisions right.

But worst of all, I hate that you can't celebrate a goal anymore. In the past, there was no better feeling than totally letting go as the ball hit the net. Scream. Shout. Lose your shit. Flick your Vs at the opposition fans. 'Eat that goal, you fuckers!' Now, you have to hold back your emotions for a VAR check. Imagine the Champions League final in 1999. Solskjaer scores the winner with the last kick of the game . . . but you can't celebrate. You just know some dweeb is going to pore over every movement in the box and look for a ridiculous way to rule the goal out.

If it was down to me, I'd totally scrap VAR. Put it in the bin where it belongs. Let's just get on with the football. From the beginning, I said it would be more trouble than it was worth. However, no matter the continued fuck ups that put the integrity of the game into question, UEFA refuse to wake up and smell the shit, even when someone is farting in their face. Whatever happens, VAR looks like it's here to stay. So, how can we fix it? Again, Goldbridge has the answers.

Firstly, we need to take some lessons from other sports. In rugby, when a decision goes to the TMO (Television Match Official), the fans can hear the referee's and the TMO's conversation in real time. The fans know exactly what's going on and can follow the process. There's none of this Michael Owen and Howard Webb nonsense, analysing the audio two weeks later. What's the point of that? Just play the audio in real time. Show the fans exactly what is going on. Remove any doubt of bias. Show the thought process. Stop passing the buck and trying to hide the crap. If rugby can do it successfully and has been doing so for years, then there's no excuse.

Full transparency shouldn't be a revolutionary idea. We're talking about getting a decision right in a football match, not asking who killed JFK!

In rugby, the TMO also has a script that must be followed. For instance, before making the final decision to award a try, the referee has to ask: 'Can I award the try?' It's bonkers such a script isn't already in place with VAR. We all heard the audio after the Luis Díaz goal. It was like listening to a group of pissed-up prats in a pub. They were as useful as a New Year's Eve party to a turkey. A set script would have eradicated any of these issues. 'Can I award a goal? Yes. It was onside.' Job fucking done. Fucking simples.

VAR is also used far too often. We need to limit it, as far as possible, to automated decisions. Keep the goal-line technology and bring in the automated offside technology that was used at the Qatar World Cup and in the Champions League. This technology is totally objective. The ball has either crossed the line or it hasn't. The player is offside or on. However, for any subjective calls, like a foul, we should follow tennis, where in each set a player has three opportunities to challenge a call. For me, that's the perfect solution. We're not stopping the game every five minutes to look at every little thing. Each manager should have three VAR calls they can contest per half. This puts some of the responsibility back on them and means that VAR can't refuse to look at something when they're told to. How often have we seen something horrendous happen and the VAR doesn't even look at it? If the managers oppose a ref's call, they can force them to look at it again like in *A Clockwork Orange*. Open your eyes, you prats. See! It's a fucking foul!

This brings me to my final way of sorting out VAR. Get people involved in the technology who actually know and understand the game. They don't need to be ex-professional players (I wouldn't trust some of these ex-pros to run a bath), but what we need are people from all walks of life who know the game. Fans, amateur managers, it doesn't matter. Let them sit with the referees in the VAR studio and give their opinion. We constantly hear referees being criticised for not knowing the game. VAR now gives us the opportunity to bring people into the decision-making process who do. Really, VAR should be a mix of everybody who knows and loves the game because that's what football is, for everyone. This way, they're not all part of the same clique, afraid of rocking the boat. Let Roy Keane loose in there. That'll sort the bastards out. 'Do your fucking job.' Alternatively, give Goldbridge a seat at the head table. I'll show you just how easy this shit is. Mic me up, you cowards.

For now, VAR is ruining the game. Most football fans I speak to hate it as well. Do any of the managers and players even like it? Or is this just another bungled idea from a bunch of suits who are totally detached from the fans? Goldbridge Check Complete. Decision: it's fucking shit.

## CHALLENGE COMPETITIONS

It's 1992. The old Wembley is holding its breath. The Manchester United and Nottingham Forest fans are there to watch the Rumbelows Cup final, but on the side of the pitch, something far more interesting is set to take place.

A group of players are lining up in their full kit and boots, but they're not there to play football. For weeks, they've been taking part in heats, broadcast on *Saint and Greavsie*, to determine who is the fastest footballer in the country. All 92 clubs in the Football League entered a candidate, many of whom were keen to win not only the accolade but also the £10,000 prize. Although, I'm not entirely sure how seriously some of the players took it.

The night before the final, Swansea's John Williams, a former postman, got hammered in his hotel and turned up looking lower than a worm's nutsack. Taking one look at the sozzled Williams, and then Notts County's Kevin Bartlett, horse-racing odds expert John McCririck proclaimed Bartlett to be the favourite, after running 11.40 in the heats. That's some going, that.

As the players took their places, some in standing position, a hush fell over the crowd before a whistle broke the silence. Suddenly, these highly toned athletes were off, pounding towards the finish line. Overcoming his hangover, John

216

Williams was the first to cross the line in just 11.49 seconds, with the much fancied Bartlett coming second. No matter what else he achieved in his career, Williams would always be known as the fastest man in football. With the money, he also bought himself a Peugeot 205 GTI 1.9. Lovely little motor, that. Good on you, John.

Sadly, this was the first and last time this race happened. Before long, Rumbelows was bust, *Saint and Greavsie* was no more and ITV lost its football coverage to Sky. I'd love to bring something like this back, though – not just a sprint challenge but an all-out football challenge extravaganza. Just hear me out.

As I mentioned before, during Arsenal's pre-season game in America, the players took part in a skills competition. I don't see why in the Premier League, maybe before the Community Shield, we can't have a series of challenges to crown who is the best at various skills in football: volleys, headers, freestyling, crossbar challenge, sprints. More people would tune in to watch Kyle Walker race Mo Salah than for an actual City vs Liverpool game.

We've actually had similar things like this before. In the 1970s there was a television show called *Superstars*. This saw top athletes from all sports compete against each other in a series of challenges. You'd see players in their prime, like Liverpool's Kevin Keegan, compete in weightlifting, sprinting, tennis, pistol shooting and even gymnastics. Although he was a regular for England and Liverpool at the time, Keegan took it very seriously, even carrying on after falling off his bike during a cycle race. Newcastle's Malcolm MacDonald even won the 100 metres, clocking in at an incredible 10.9 seconds, a *Superstars* record – and almost quick enough to be an Olympic qualifying time that year.

This is just the stuff I want to see. It would certainly end a few debates in the pub and dressing rooms as well.

## SIX-A-SIDE

Imagine a six-a-side team with European Cup winners George Best, Sir Bobby Charlton, Alex Stepney and David Sadler, all playing in a tournament in the prime of their careers. Sounds bloody good, doesn't it? This actually happened in 1970, when United took part in the National *Daily Express* Five-a-Side Competition at Wembley Arena in front of 10,000 fans. Unsurprisingly, with that lineup, United won the tournament, with Best scoring both goals in the final to defeat Spurs. Go on, Bestie!

This wasn't a one-off, either. The tournament was played every November from 1968 to 1986. During this time, it featured some of the greats, such as Bryan Robson, Charlie Nicholas, Kevin Keegan, Glenn Hoddle and Sir Geoff Hurst. And they weren't there to just fuck about, either. This was no exhibition game. This was serious stuff. In 1969 Manchester City's Colin Bell took part just a day after appearing for England in Amsterdam. The fans loved it as well. The arena was always sold out and the games were even broadcast on the BBC.

This was all slightly before my time, but I do recall another annual competition in the late eighties called Soccer Six, which was organised by the Football League and held at Manchester's G-Mex arena. It was on TV before Christmas, and all the top-flight clubs entered teams. As if that wasn't enough, the opening credits were set to 'Eye of the Tiger'. You're dead inside if that doesn't get your blood pumping.

With English clubs banned from Europe for five years from 1985 due to the Heysel disaster, this became a major competition. It wasn't something for the kids or reserves. You put out the full arsenal at your disposal. For instance, title-winning Everton took the tournament so seriously the club's Soccer Six squad included Neville Southall, Kevin Ratcliffe, Pat Van Den Hauwe, Dave Watson, Peter Reid, Trevor Steven, Tony Cottee and Graeme Sharp.

With this much talent on display, it was incredible to watch. The games were quicker and a lot more skill was involved, with players having to beat each other in more limited space. The ball also never went out of play, so it was frantic, and with smaller pitches, there were also far more goals. You could thunderbastard it in from anywhere.

The dream didn't last long, though. By the time English clubs were readmitted to Europe in 1990, ready to be destroyed by random Russian teams, the tournament was scrapped. For a few years, six-a-side was in the wilderness until Sky broadcast Masters games. This consisted of retired 'legends' aged over 35 representing their former clubs. It was good fun, and I enjoyed watching it when it was on, although the term 'legend' was clearly applied very loosely. In some cases, it seemed even a one-time kit man might get a game. Still, nothing was funnier than watching a former pro, who'd clearly been at the biscuit tin since they'd packed it in, huffing and puffing their way around the pitch, trying to reclaim former glories. But every so often, one of them would turn back the clock and prove they still had it.

I still love watching clips of retired pros playing six-a-side. If you go on YouTube, there are some incredible clips of the likes of Ronaldinho or Francesco Totti absolutely destroying people. There are also some amazing clips of current Juventus striker Dušan Vlahović when he was younger taking no prisoners. Still, it's no match for players in their prime taking part in a competition that matters.

I'd love to watch this today. An annual Premier League six-a-side tournament. This would be a load of fun in itself but I'd also like to see who would win, as it would be very different from the 11-a-side game. The easy money would, of course, be on City. They'd be formidable with Ederson in goal, Stones and Walker at the back, De Bruyne and Silva in midfield and Haaland up front. Although, I think Spurs could be dark horses, with Vicario in goal, Romero and Van de Ven in defence, Bissouma and Maddison in midfield, and Son up front. I like the mix of that team. Like City, it has a bit of everything. I can't even face doing a United one. As soon as I get to Maguire and Evans as centre backs, I know it's already over. Still, I bet Bruno would be incredible at six-a-side. He could twat it in from anywhere.

For me, the ideal time to play would be the two weeks before Christmas, just like Soccer Six used to do. A day of festive Premier League six-a-side would be epic. Stick that on the list, please, Santa.

## MIXED TEAMS

The women's game has exploded in recent years, culminating with the Lionesses winning the European Championships in 2022. I was so proud, but better still, my daughter loved it. She'd always followed football, but now she had her own heroes to inspire her.

Growing up, women's football just wasn't a thing. It wasn't encouraged and, looking back, women weren't really welcomed into the game. That's all changed now, and it's been wonderful to watch it go from strength to strength, making huge strides in a short amount of time. While I'm sure women want to focus on growing their own game, especially as it has had such success, I'm also sure that one day, we will have women play in the men's professional game. Sit down, Joey Barton. You're not on *Question Time* now. Just listen and learn.

The men's game is obviously more physical and quicker, but the top women players can be just as technically good as men. Chelsea men's captain Reece James certainly thinks so. His sister Lauren plays for Chelsea in the Women's Super League as well as for England, and he thinks she's better than some Premier League players. Her exquisite double against China in the 2023 World Cup certainly suggested she could hold her own.

Maybe James is slightly biased, but I'm also sure that the skill level in the women's game is getting there. The standard has come on leaps and bounds in just a few short years and will only improve. Just think of the smaller, less physical players who have thrived in the men's game over the years: Juninho, Kinkladze, Zola, David Silva, to name just a few. I'm certain that a female player will play in the Premier League one day, especially at the rate women's football is progressing.

Until then, I'd love to see a competition with mixed teams. Perhaps, the top men's and women's players for each club joining forces and playing against each other for a charity match or a good cause. Forget Boehly's north vs south all-star game. I'd much rather watch this. Reece James and Lauren James joining forces for Chelsea; Rachel Daly and Ollie Watkins terrorising defences for Villa; Bunny Shaw lining up alongside Erling Haaland for City. I'm sure it would also help to continue to advance the women's game, which is no bad thing. It might even show that the women can more than hold their own against the men.


## THINGS WE'VE LOST


'I've seen things you people wouldn't believe . . . All those moments will be lost in time, like tears in rain . . .'

Rutger Hauer's monologue from *Blade Runner* is one of my favourite film scenes of all time. He plays Roy Batty, a replicant (cyborg), talking about all of the incredible things he's seen in the few years he's been alive that will soon be forgotten when he dies. I often feel like this as a football fan. Change can be good. But along the way, it also means having to say goodbye to things we have loved, that have been a part of the fabric of the game and our lives. Special moments that have been and gone, never to be replaced, such as standing in the pissing rain outside a Dixons on a Saturday afternoon.

Before the days of the internet, if you were out and about on a Saturday afternoon you couldn't just look at your phone for the latest scores or results. No such luck, pal. The internet wasn't even invented then. Or if it was, we certainly weren't carrying it around in our pockets. If you wanted to know the football results, you had to get yourself sharpish to an electrical store.

On Saturdays at 4.45pm, in town centres up and down the land, football fans would spontaneously and magically gather outside the likes of Radio Rentals, Rumbelows or Dixons. Staring through the display windows, they'd watch the television screens, switched to *Grandstand* for the football results. This was one of the great sights of the eighties and nineties. In high streets up and down the country, no matter the weather, there'd be a large group of men, usually each with a cigarette in their mouth, oooohing, sighing or merely nodding their head as each result came up on the screen.

Those shops also knew exactly what they were doing. It was the best free marketing they could ask for. It encouraged hordes of football supporters to gather in front of the shop to take in the results and hopefully feel so euphoric that they'd pop in for a new television while they were at it. Free enterprise at its best.

Back then, football wasn't the monster it is today. Of course, it was still popular, but it was also a bit like a secret tribe. Because of hooliganism, there was a bit of shame attached to publicly declaring you were a football supporter. People wouldn't necessarily think that you were a harmless fan of Blackpool. They'd assume you were armed to the teeth with switchblades and knuckle-dusters, running with a hooligan firm. Therefore, seeing these men come out of the shadows at 4.45pm and gather together in public, away from the terraces, was a bit special. Supporters of all clubs would put down their weapons and come together for this weekly ritual.

If you couldn't get near a television, there was another way to get all the results: the *Football Post*. All regions had a version of this. It was basically a newspaper, usually pink, which was totally dedicated to the football news and results. Incredibly, it would hit the shops around an hour and a half after the game had finished. I took this for granted at the time but thinking of it now, it blows my mind. Just think about it for a moment. Immediately after the final whistle, journalists at games around the country would have to write and send in their match reports to the newspaper's head office. Remember, there was no internet. Often, these match reports would be read to a secretary over the phone so they could be typed up. Even then, they'd still need to be formatted and accompanying photographs would also need to have been sent in and placed appropriately. With this all done, the paper would then be sent to press so it could be printed in its thousands, collected by a van and then distributed to newsagents across the county, all within 90 minutes of the game having finished. Ninety minutes! This happened every single week. It's one of the great modern miracles, like Marcus Rashford suddenly playing well before a contract renewal.

Fixtures also weren't spread out like they are today. Back then, virtually all games across the Football League kicked off at 3pm on a Saturday. There was, therefore, something sacred about the 3pm Saturday kick-off. It was a time set aside to totally devote yourself to football. The fact that we didn't have phones showing us clips of the goals or controversial moments all added to the drama. You might get the text flash up during *Grandstand* saying, 'Vinnie Jones sent off,' or read in the *Football Post* that Efan Ekoku had scored four at Goodison, but that's all you'd know until you watched *Match of the Day* later that night. As for who got the assist? Well, assists were like the Loch Ness Monster back in those days. They didn't exist.

It's no wonder as many as 12 million people used to regularly tune in to *Match of the Day*. It was such an institution. You'd been drip-fed news of the games all day from *Grandstand*, the *Football Post*, maybe even radio commentary or a phone-in show. However, *Match of the Day* was the first time most of us could actually see what had happened with our own eyes. Your parents would make you go to bed at 8pm on weeknights. But on Saturday, parents were having a laugh if they thought that was going to fly. Saturday night was all geared up for Des Lynam, Alan Hansen, Trevor Brooking and Mark Lawrenson. Being allowed to stay up late added to the magic of it all. And then the iconic theme music would kick in . . . Duh duh duh duh duh duh duh duh duh . . . duh duh

duh duh duh duh. Go on. Admit it, you've been humming along. We're in a safe place here. Let yourself go.

I would sit alongside my grandad as we finally saw footage of David Beckham scoring from the halfway line. Having to wait to see it made the goal even more special. It wasn't something disposable. Something you could watch in ten seconds on your phone then put away and go about your day. You'd had hours to build up this moment in your head. You'd conjure up all the ways the goal had been scored, the reaction of the crowd, even the celebration. The anticipation to see the goal would kill you. And you knew that millions of football supporters around the country were all watching it at the same time as you. It was like when *Star Wars* would be shown on Christmas Day in the years when there were only four channels. It was event television.

These days, most of us get the results via our phone, on social media or from one of the many football apps out there. You don't just get the results anymore, either. There's footage of the goals to go along with it, as well as video match reports. Don't get me wrong. I love all of this, but I feel like we're missing something. However, there is still a way to sample some of this nostalgia.

If you happen to walk through a department store electrical department at 4.45pm on a Saturday, you might still get a small gathering of people surrounding a television as the results come in. If you see these hardy souls keeping tradition alive, then go and join them, maybe even strike up a conversation and revel in one of football's great pastimes. If you're feeling ultra generous, take a packet of Werther's Original with you and share them out. God, it makes me all misty-eyed. Bloody football, hey?

# 8

# HAVE A BREAK
# FROM YOUR CLUB

Alright, deep breath, Mark. Just rip the plaster off. It'll all be OK. Don't get triggered. This is why some of the knobheads are here. Give them what they want. Here we go . . .

We were seconds away from winning the title. The United players and Sir Alex were out on the pitch, ready to go bloody mental after a 1–0 win at Sunderland. Better still, our noisy neighbours had bottled it. They were losing 2–1 at the Etihad to relegation-threatened QPR, managed by United legend Mark Hughes. Bloody fantastic. With just seconds remaining, even a draw wouldn't be enough for them to win the title. All season, City had been crowing that this was their year. This was the season that the club would win its first title since 1968 and finally topple United from the top.

*Ooooo, we're a big club now. Look at us and our tippy-tappy football. Ooooo.*

Get back in that fucking bin. You've bottled it more times than a Coca-Cola factory. Have some of that, ya twats. Shut up and sit down. It really couldn't have panned out any better. It was all my Christmases at once.

I was about to pour myself a celebratory Diet Coke and toast our fifth title in six years when Eden Džeko equalised for City in the 92nd minute. Bless him. Shove it up your arse, Džeko, you still need another goal, pal, and there are only seconds left. I actually chuckled to myself. They'd lose the title by one goal. I couldn't have scripted it better myself. But then the ball broke to Balotelli on the edge of the box. He poked it towards Agüero as the QPR defence scattered like a bunch of pigeons, and then . . . Yeah, you know what happened next. We're not going to describe it. Alright. Shut up and sit down. Bunch of bloody rubberneckers. Don't fist the air. Fist yourselves.

After this debacle, I refused to watch football for the next three months. I avoided it like Jadon Sancho in a narrow Carrington corridor with Erik ten Hag. 'No thanks. I'll go the other way.' But it was fucking hard. All summer long, I had to avoid the replays. Martin Tyler shouting, 'Can you believe what you're seeing.' Fuck. That. Shit. My eyes are bleached. Get that shite away from me. It made me want to throw up.

Being a United fan, we've had tremendous periods of dominance and won plenty of trophies. Yet, like that City game, there are still a few that can keep me up at night wondering, *How the chuffing hell did we fuck that up?* Drawing at West Ham in 1995 to hand the title to Blackburn, after they'd lost at Anfield. Losing the 1995 FA Cup final to Everton, who had spent most of the season playing like they wanted to get relegated. Then there's the Champions League final loss to Barcelona in Rome in 2009. I was so convinced we would win that game that in the lead-up I bought a T-shirt with 'The Italian Job' emblazoned across it. I know. I know. What did you expect, Goldbridge? You great big prat. You're bantering yourself. But that's how convinced I was that we were going to win. We had won the Champions League final just a year previously, and Ronaldo and Rooney were on fire. It felt like the start of a United dynasty.

Instead, the 2009 final was the birth of that great Barca team, one of the greatest of all time. Messi, Iniesta and Xavi played a different sport to the rest of us back then. God, Messi was brilliant. We were like a bunch of drunk sailors trying to swat a fly. We lost 2–0 and never got close to them. We had been totally dicked on. That's what made it hurt all the more. I had been so caught up in United having a great team that I had failed to recognise that Barca was more than our equal. I couldn't sleep that night. The T-shirt was a waste of money as well. Twenty quid down the drain. I used it to wash the car for a bit, but I eventually had to bin it as I couldn't stand looking at it. I like washing the car. It's relaxing. But looking at that shite would just set me off full Goldbridge.

Every football fan has memories like these, of a time when your club has fucked you so badly that you're scarred by the experience. Just think of poor Peterborough fans. After the first leg of the 2023 League One play-off semi-finals, The Posh were 4–0 up against Sheffield Wednesday. Book your tickets to Wembley, lads. This one is done and dusted. Get in that Travelodge before it's fully booked. But in the second leg, they were like mice going after cheese in a mousetrap. Time and time again, they poured forward, only to concede. Use your bloody noggins, lads. Stop going for the cheese. They couldn't be stopped, though. Bloody greedy bastards. They drew the second leg 5–5 on aggregate and then went out on penalties. How has that even happened? It shouldn't even be possible. It's the sort of shite that makes you want to tell football to swivel on it and fuck off.

Now, let's not be silly here. We all think football is the greatest sport on earth. We don't need to go full David Bentley and walk away from it completely. Sometimes you've got to hold your hands up, though. It's Ivan Drago. You're Apollo Creed. And Rocky won't throw in that damn towel. You've taken enough punches. You need to take a break from your club's shitshow. Let me show you how. Come on. It'll be alright.

## GARETH SOUTHGATE'S BARMY ARMY

I was just ten years old, and I was sobbing my little bloody heart out. Chris Waddle had just blazed his penalty over the bar in the 1990 World Cup semi-final as if it was sponsored by NASA. The West German players in green flooded the pitch as our gallant heroes in white sunk to their knees. While my grandad and uncles cursed at the television, I stared in shock, tears in my eyes. *What the fucking fuck is this?*

The previous few weeks had changed my life. For the first time I had become engrossed in an international tournament. I'd never witnessed a full World Cup before England kicked off against Ireland, but soon I was hooked. Gary Lineker was the nation's golden boy, and we all loved him, even if he did poo his pants, but Gazza was the naughty kid in school you wanted to be your friend. It was like watching a child play with the big kids. I loved him sticking his tongue out during the national anthem, mouthing 'Fucking wanker' instead of saying 'Paul Gascoigne' in the pre-match television segment when they announced the team, having a cake thrown into his face on his birthday, and playing tennis against American tourists just hours before a big game.

Along with all of that was the skill and the ability to do it on the biggest stage of all. We were witnessing greatness.

When he pulled out a Cruyff turn against the Dutch, sending two defenders in the opposite direction, I almost fell out of my chair. 'What the bloody hell was that?' I shouted. No one knew. He might as well have come from Mars.

Everything about that summer was magical. As England pulled off late heroics against Egypt, Belgium and Cameroon, the hot weather back home matched the mood. It was a bright new dawn. For years the English national team had been as useless as tits on a nun. We didn't even qualify for the 1974 and 1978 World Cups. In 1982 we somehow went undefeated and still found ourselves knocked out. And then there was 1986, with that colossal cheating prick Maradona. Club football wasn't doing much better, either. After the Heysel disaster in 1985, English clubs were banned from Europe for five years. Then came the Hillsborough disaster in April 1989. Football in England was in terminal decline. Yet, just a year later, this vibrant England team, with a mix of loveable characters, led by the wonderful Sir Bobby Robson, was sticking it to the world's best. It was hard not to get carried away, and by heck, we did. This was liquid football, and we all wanted a creamy cold pint.

Every time you put on the radio, John Barnes was rapping on 'World in Motion' or Luciano Pavarotti was belting out 'Nessun dorma'. That still gives me shivers to this day. The BBC's opening credits to its World Cup coverage were also the best ever. Absolutely fantastic. After every game, the hysteria kept building and building. Everyone in the country was transfixed. Grandparents, parents, children and pets were all willing the team on together.

I knew something special was happening because not only was I allowed to stay up late to watch the games, but so were all my friends. In the glorious sunshine, during break times, we'd emulate Gazza, Lineker, Platt, Barnes and Waddle. After another heroic performance against Cameroon, it just seemed inevitable that England was going to go all the way. Things this good can't be stopped. Not even an excellent West German team, boasting the likes of Lothar Matthäus and Jürgen Klinsmann, could get in the way. Gazza and Lineker would surely swipe them aside, setting up a final against Argentina and the world's greatest player (and cheat) Diego Maradona. The stage was set after his Hand of God had knocked England out of the 1986 World Cup. Revenge and redemption would be sweet. Have some of that, ya cheating bastard!

So, with all of this in mind, when England battled through to a penalty shoot-out against West Germany, there was no way we could lose. We had done things the hard way against Cameroon and emerged victorious. This was just another moment of high drama that would make our eventual victory all the sweeter. Then Stuart Pearce had his penalty saved. No worries. Peter Shilton will save one. But he didn't. He didn't even get close. For fuck's sake, Shilton. He was diving around like he was falling off the sofa. Now it fell on Chris Waddle to score to keep us alive. And he put the ball right over the fucking bar. I'm telling you now that ball is still in space. You're never getting that back.

That miss was the first time I realised the world wasn't fair. We don't live in a film where you're guaranteed a happy ending. Father Christmas and the Tooth Fairy aren't real. Bad things can happen when you least expect it. It was a full-force slap in the face, like being Tango'd. (Good adverts, them. I can see why they were banned, though. You don't see Tango much anymore, come to think of it. Decent beverage.)

Anyway, the story repeated itself six years later, and muggins here fell for it all over again. Another hot summer, Three Lions on repeat, a Gazza wondergoal against the Scots, Shearer destroying the Dutch at Wembley, Pearce going ballistic in the penalty shoot-out win against Spain. Once more, victory seemed inevitable, particularly as this was the first tournament in England since 1966, when we had last become world champions.

Playing Germany in the semi-finals at Wembley seemed the perfect stage for glorious revenge. When we took an early lead, thanks to a Shearer header, it just felt inevitable that football was indeed coming fucking home. Then the appropriately named Kuntz equalised, and the game went to extra time. With the golden goal rule in play, Darren Anderton hit the post and Gazza was a toenail's length away from tapping the ball into an empty net. I still don't know how that didn't go in. Seriously. It's a joke. A penalty shoot-out beckoned.

The innocence of youth had been flattened in 1990. However, once again, I fooled myself that it was all going to be OK. Every movie has an 'all is lost' moment, just before the triumphant third act. I thought that Italia 90 was our 'all is lost' and Euro 96 was the final act, where our heroes had learned from their mistakes and could defeat the mighty foe. At Wembley, there was no more fitting place to do it. Everything seemed set for an almighty redemption story, particularly when Stuart Pearce smashed his penalty home, atoning for his miss in 1990. Then Gareth bloody Southgate stepped forward . . .

For fuck's sake, Gareth! If you're shitting yourself, just put your foot through it.

Again, I watched the television, barely comprehending what I had seen. It felt like my guts had been ripped out. I half-expected an alien to emerge and start singing show tunes like in *Spaceballs*. The villains had triumphed at the end of the second act, as well as the third. Who's writing this bloody script? It's like an episode of *EastEnders*. Have some misery, and then have some fucking more. *Les Misérables* and then some. Kuntz!

As the years went by, England continued to follow the same script as Ian Beale. Every major tournament saw the team fuck it up in ever more dramatic fashion. There was Beckham and Rooney getting sent off, more missed penalties, major injuries at crucial times (we all know what a metatarsal is now) and the feeling that referees were robbing us blind. Sol Campbell's disallowed goals against Argentina in 1998 and Portugal in 2004 were particularly bad. Frank Lampard's shot against Germany in 2010, hitting the underside of the bar and going at least a yard over the line and still not being given, was bloody criminal. By then I was numb to it all, hardened by years of disappointment. I vowed never to get fooled again.

Even when England reached the final of Euro 2020, and played Italy at Wembley, I didn't let myself get carried away. So, when Rashford, Sancho and Saka all missed their penalties, I didn't stand in front of the television, tears rolling down my cheeks, as I had done in 1990. I was still bloody pissed off – I mean, we missed three penalties in a row – but deep down, it just felt inevitable.

There was also something else. Something that I hadn't really admitted to myself all this time. England didn't deserve to win any of those tournaments. We wouldn't have been worthy winners. Sure, we had a great team with some legendary players, but we still weren't the best. Germany was better. Brazil was better. France was better. Spain was better. Italy was better. We weren't convincing like those sides were. We didn't control games like they could. We always seemed short in one or two positions or had a great first 11 but not a great squad.

I look back at the so-called Golden Generation between 2001 and 2004, which we all thought would conquer the world. There's no denying that, on paper, we had a first 11 packed with world-class talent. In goal, there was David Seaman, a back four of Ashley Cole, Rio Ferdinand, John Terry and Gary Neville, a midfield of Beckham, Scholes, Gerrard and Lampard, and a front two of Owen and Rooney. I grant you, it looks a hell of a team. Yet despite all of that talent, we never had the right balance. The biggest issue was the midfield. All four of those midfield players were world-class, but they were far too similar to play together. But who would you drop? Sven-Göran Eriksson ended up playing Paul Scholes on the left wing. That's like asking Robert De Niro to do panto with Jonathan Wilkes at the Regent Theatre in Stoke. What a waste. He then asked one of Gerrard or Lampard to play as a holding midfielder. It's no wonder we always got overrun in midfield when up against the best. Still, that team should have at least reached the semi-finals of a major tournament. They massively underachieved.

So, after all of these horror stories, why am I advocating that you take a break from the horrors of club football and switch your allegiance to England? Because I still believe. That's right. I do. Maybe now more than ever. The story's not over yet.

Going into Euro 2024, it feels like this is the best chance in my lifetime for England to finally win a major tournament, ending 58 years of hurt (almost double the amount of time Baddiel and Skinner complained about!). As things currently stand, the England squad is the envy of the world. It's packed with talent. It pains me to say it, but Manchester City are the current champions of Europe, with the likes of John Stones, Kyle Walker, Phil Foden and Jack Grealish coached by one of the best managers of all time. These aren't just good Premier League players; they would get picked for most club and national sides in world football. Then there's the real stardust: Jude Bellingham and Harry Kane. England now boasts one of the best midfielders in world football, the poster boy for Real Madrid. Spearheading the attack, we have the nation's record goal scorer, World Cup Golden Boot winner and Bayern Munich's record-breaking number 9. We've never had it so good.

Along with the stand-out talent, we also have some exceptional Premier League players: Bukayo Saka, James Maddison, Cole Palmer, Marcus Rashford, Declan Rice, Reece James, Luke Shaw. The list goes on and on. The best thing of all is that most of these players are still young yet already have plenty of international experience. They've grown together through the heartache of Euro 2020 and then Qatar 2022. This has all been a learning curve. We will now see the best of this young England side in the tournaments to come.

Like I said, we've had good England sides in the past, but other countries have just been better. But not now, and certainly not in Europe. I mean, come on. Let's look at the usual suspects. Germany is currently all over the shop. They got beat 4–1 by Japan at home in September 2023, for fuck's sake, and that was their fourth defeat in five games. Spain always has some talent, but their squad is currently very thin. The same goes for Italy, who failed to qualify for Qatar 2022 after losing to North Macedonia in the play-offs! The only real threat right now comes from France, which has Kylian Mbappé leading the line, along with the likes of Eduardo Camavinga, Aurélien Tchouaméni and Antoine Griezmann, to name just a few others in their talent-filled squad. I grant you, they're a good team. A very good team. But I still don't think they have a squad as strong as England's.

I'm convinced that England can only lose by beating themselves, like a drunk punching himself in the face. The talent, experience and youth are all there like never before. Now, everyone knows my opinion on Gareth Southgate – a nice man who has been found tactically wanting at the highest level. Having your manager as your greatest weakness isn't the best. But they say insanity is doing the same thing over and over again and expecting a different result. Like the players, Southgate has also been learning about top-level international football over the last few tournaments. He now has a wealth of experience that no England manager has ever had before. Surely, he has learned some valuable lessons and won't make the same mistakes again. Will you, Gareth? Come on now. Don't fuck this up. If Roberto Di Matteo can manage a team to win the Champions League, even you can manage this England team to glory.

So, if your club side is currently getting you down, go all in for England. Yes, we are scarred. We've been hurt too many times before. It's hard to trust our high hopes again. But let it go. Forget Italia 90, Euro 96 and the rest. Most players in this squad weren't even born when those tournaments took place, and those who were certainly won't remember them. It's time for a fresh new dawn. To heal from the past trauma. When England finally get over the line – and they will – then we're all going to have one big fucking party.

SWEET CAROLINE! GOOD TIMES NEVER SEEMED SO GOOD! SO GOOD! SO BLOODY GOOD!

## GAZZETTA FOOTBALL ITALIA

In the 1990s, Serie A was the best league in the world. Nowhere else was comparable. It might even be the best league of all time. During this time, Italian teams won 13 of the 30 European titles available and had 25 finalists! Throw in six world-record transfers and six Ballon d'Or winners, and it really was a different gravy.

It wasn't just two or three clubs stockpiling all the talent like you might get today, either. Almost every team boasted world-class players in their prime. AC Milan had the likes of Gullit, Rijkaard, Van Basten, Maldini and Weah. Juventus had

Zidane, Davids and Del Piero. Inter had Ronaldo, Baggio, Zamorano and Vieri. Fiorentina boasted Batistuta and Rui Costa. Parma had Crespo, Veron, Thuram, Cannavaro and Buffon. I mean, for fuck's sake!

Then there was the English contingent. After Italia 90, Gazza joined Lazio, David Platt joined Bari and Des Walker signed for Sampdoria. Later on, Paul Ince joined Inter Milan and Lee Sharpe went on loan to Sampdoria. Unsurprisingly, everyone wanted to watch Serie A. Thankfully, Channel 4 heard the call.

In 1992, they started broadcasting *Gazzetta Football Italia*. Bloody hell, it was good. On Saturday mornings, presenter James Richardson would sit outside a café in some square in Rome, the Italian newspapers spread across the table, an exotic Italian gelato and a coffee at the ready, and then go over the previous week's action. Usually, Gazza would make an appearance as well, most memorably shitting himself while holding a snake at a zoo. I mean, that's just top-quality programming. We're a bit short on content this week, lads. Fuck it, let's take Gazza to the zoo. No wonder I jacked in *Going Live* and *Gordon the Gopher* for it. So did plenty of others. More than 800,000 people a week were tuning in. It became Channel 4's most-watched Saturday morning show ever.

As if that wasn't enough, on Sunday afternoons, the channel would show a live Italian game. At the time, this was as good as football got. It was all so exotic. The players also looked cooler. They had long hair, funny little goatees and sideburns, different boots, and often looked like they'd stepped off the catwalk. It was quite jarring to watch Serie A and then switch over to the Premier League to watch Neil Ruddock and Vinnie Jones go head-to-head. The difference in standards was astonishing.

The best thing about all of this? You could watch football and enjoy it. Sure, you might have a favourite Italian side – most chose Lazio because of Gazza – but you weren't as invested in the game as you were when it was your club side. There were no nerves. No feeling of dread. No eye-rolling thoughts of *Here we fucking go again*. It was all good vibes. Stick on Sheryl Crow, 'All I Wanna Do Is Have Some Fun'. You might get a little disappointed if your team lost, but by then it was time for the Sunday roast and back to the Premier League, with your palate refreshed and your belly full.

Since the glory days, when *Gazzetta Football* whetted our appetite for foreign football, we've had no shortage of choices. After David Beckham signed for Real Madrid in 2003, Sky broadcast La Liga games. While it was great to follow Beckham and the Galacticos and watch Ronaldinho, Henry and Eto rip it up at Barca, you also got to witness the emergence of one of the great club sides of all time. Pep Guardiola's 'tiki-taka' side of 2008–12 takes some beating. With Messi, Xavi and Iniesta all in their prime, Barcelona blew most teams away.

Then there was the Luis Enrique Barca team of 2014–17, with an attacking trio of Messi, Neymar and Suárez going toe-to-toe with Zidane's Madrid team of Ronaldo, Bale and Benzema. It's no wonder both teams dominated Europe with attacks like that. Again, it was a joy to watch. We didn't know how good we had it. Never again will we have two generational talents like Messi and Ronaldo, going toe-to-toe for rival teams in the same league, with both producing such astonishing results.

Since Ronaldo and Messi have departed Spain, La Liga has lost some of its lustre in recent years. But there's no shortage of football to watch from other leagues around the world. You only have to go on YouTube or subscription-based streaming services to watch games from the MLS, Germany, France, Saudi Arabia, South America and more.

So, if you're sick to death of your team or the circus that surrounds the Premier League, support a team from another part of the world. If this doesn't float your boat though, you could just walk to your local park. Growing up, I spent Saturday afternoons watching my grandad manage a local amateur team. It was far from professional standard, but I loved it. In the changing room, laughing at the banter flying back and forth, cheering the goals on the side of a muddy pitch and chatting about the game afterwards in the car on the way home: to me, it was all just as magical as being at Old Trafford. Whether it's your children's team, or even some random strangers, park football is the bedrock of the sport in this country. Get out in the fresh air, soak it up and remind yourself why you fell in love with this beautiful game in the first place.

## PICK ANOTHER SPORT

To some, this is blasphemous, but sometimes it all gets too much. It's not just your club that's getting you down, but football as a whole. We all know it's the greatest sport in the world. And yet, we also have to hold our hands up and admit it's not perfect. The violence and racism are nowhere near as bad as they used to be, but they're still there. As I write, a Newcastle fan has been stabbed in Milan, and Tottenham wingback Destiny Udogie has been racially abused on social media. Then, there are the frequent scandals – Greenwood, Antony, Mendy, Giggs – not to mention the petulance of astonishingly well-paid players throwing their toys out of the pram or not training hard enough. That's before you even get to your team ruining another weekend with a clusterfuck of a performance. It all leaves a bad taste in your mouth. You know you'll never leave football. You'll always come crawling back. But sometimes, a break can do you some good.

No matter the sport, I've always loved watching world-class athletes compete against each other. Growing up, my hero was tennis legend Andre Agassi. Not only was he a great tennis player, but he stood out from the pack with his hoop earring, flowing mullet and technicolour cycling shorts. (Although I was shocked to learn, years later, that this magnificent mullet was in fact a wig! Hell of a hairpiece, Andre my old son.) I've always liked a rebel, particularly one who can back it up with talent. That's one of the reasons I love George Best and Gazza. Better still, I love rooting for a rebel against a poster boy. At the time, the poster boy of tennis was the clean-cut all-American Pete Sampras. Watching the two go head to head was exhilarating.

Sampras was like a cyborg, a winning machine made in a laboratory who looked and acted the part. Agassi was the total reverse. He veered between genius and playing like some bloke with amnesia who was handed a racket and told to swing it. In 1997 Agassi even fell to 141st in the world rankings. In fairness, he later revealed that he was on meth at the time. To be on meth and still play professional sport takes some doing. I wonder if some United players have been on meth over the last decade. Joking. Drug testing is very stringent in football these days. Just ask Rio. However, in 1999 Agassi was back. After winning the French Open, he became only the fifth player to win all four Grand Slams. Once again, he was the top-ranked player in the world. I found this thrilling. When Agassi was on, he was unplayable. When he was off, he was a shambles. Still, I tuned in as often as I could. Anything could happen.

It was the same with Jonah Lomu and the New Zealand rugby team in 1995. I was no great rugby fan. I barely watched a game before that year's World Cup, but Lomu was a freak of nature. Standing at six foot four inches, he weighed almost 19 stone and could run a hundred metres in 11.2 seconds. Rugby had never seen his like before. South Africa might have won the tournament in '95 and had their own emotional ride to victory, but for me, it was always about Lomu. With a mixture of pace and power, he moved like a ballerina, waltzing away from tackles or steamrollering over them. When New Zealand faced England in the semi-finals, he virtually ran over poor Mike Catt on his way to scoring four tries. There was never any danger of me becoming a rugby fan, but I always kept an eye out for Lomu.

These days, my alternative sport of choice is the NFL. While I struggle to watch many regular season or play-off games because they're on so late in the UK, I always tune in for the Super Bowl. Again, it's the best versus the best, which I always love. I know that for that one night of the year, I'll stay up all night, load myself up with American candy and drinks, and enjoy the game. In recent years, I've even done watch-alongs for it, which has been amazing.

While I enjoy all of this, I also find myself learning from other sports. As I already mentioned, the way rugby has used the TMO is far better than VAR in football. But it's not just the on-field stuff I learn from. It's the fans from other sports as well. For instance, NFL fans love tailgate parties. Before a game, the fans gather in the stadium car park, open the tailgates to their trucks, pull out a BBQ and some beers and have a party. Why hasn't this become a thing over here? If we have to take the Kardashians from America, can't we at least import tailgate parties as well? It'd certainly beat the food at Old Trafford and probably cost a lot less as well.

## MALLETT'S MALLET

By any traditional standards, I didn't cover myself in glory during my GCSEs. Truth be told, I failed the fucking lot. I know you're surprised, aren't you? So was my fucking mum, let me tell you. But if they were handing out awards for football knowledge, I would have been top of the class.

During media studies, I used to sit with four of my mates who were also football fans. I don't know why we didn't pay attention to the class, because it discussed stuff we loved from film and television. Yet that all came a distant second to football. Instead of actually listening to the class, we'd have football quizzes. Like Mallett's Mallet, one of us would be the quizmaster while the others would have to name all the players from a particular team. This was way before the internet and smartphones. You'd just have to know your stuff or get twatted over the head. I might have been failing every class but I was immense at this. Name the Wimbledon team of 1995. No problem. This is all so ingrained in my memory I could probably still reel off the whole squad today. And back then, it wasn't even my job to know this stuff. I might have been a Manchester United fan, but more than anything, I just loved football.

A big part of this was my Panini sticker album. I got my first one in 1989, and it became an obsession. It also helped that, with my mum going through a divorce, she was probably keen to spoil me a bit. She didn't have much money, but she'd treat me to five packs of stickers every Friday night. Suddenly, I knew far more about football than just the players who played for Manchester United. It all fed into my love for the game. I found myself rooting for the most random players because I knew them from my sticker album. For instance, I'd be delighted if Robert Rosario scored for Norwich.

The best thing of all was being able to swap stickers with your mates. It meant we were all talking about football and learning together. When I was living at my grandparents' house, my uncle also still lived there. He was only a few years older than me and was also massively into football and stickers. You'd think that would make it easy to swap with each other. You'd be wrong.

For some reason, I loved Franz Carr. He was by no means a cool, big-name player. He certainly wasn't a Bryan Robson or Ian Rush. I just liked him because he had a cool name. At the time, my uncle had three Franz Carr stickers, so I tried to broker a swap deal with him. I should have known better. I was always getting mugged off in swap deals. I would have been around nine at the time, and he was 14, so he knew a lot more about football than me. If I had Gazza, he would persuade me to swap it for a random Charlton player, as apparently this guy was going to be the best player in the world. I fell for crap like this all the time. Hook, line and bloody sinker. But as he already had Franz Carr in his album and two spares, I at least thought we could come to an agreement. No bloody chance. Rather than swap a sticker I really wanted, he stuck the two spares on top of the one he already had. It's more than thirty years on, and I've still not forgotten this act of treachery. I was fuming. It cuts me deep. I never did get a Franz Carr sticker in the end, either.

Along with stickers in the 1990s, I also loved the sudden influx of football videos released around Christmas. Every year, I'd usually find the latest Danny Baker or Nick Hancock videos under the tree, or ones that focused on the great Brazilian sides, or in which Bobby Charlton would talk about the history of the World Cup. However, not all of them focused on the beautiful side of the game. The FA banned Vinnie Jones's *Soccer's Hard Men* video after he revealed some of the tricks of his trade, such as elbowing players when going up for a header or raking his studs across the opposition player's Achilles. Seriously Vinnie, what the fuck were you thinking? Unsurprisingly, the FA weren't amused. For this, he received the then-highest fine in FA history, a whopping £20,000. He only made £1,600 from making the bloody video! Despite this, many of these videos focused on great players, goals or games from the past. I lapped it all up as if I were studying for a PhD in football. This was the first time I saw Ronnie Radford's goal for Hereford in the FA Cup or Ernie Hunt's donkey kick for Coventry.

This helped give me a wider appreciation and love for the game. I wasn't just a one-eyed United fan who thought all other teams were rubbish, like so many knobheads you see on social media. I wanted to learn and consume it all. This allowed me to enjoy every game. Technically, it also should have won me some bloody money.

Armed with such vast football knowledge, I should feel like Marty McFly with a sports almanac in *Back to the Future Part II*. Unlike Marty Mcfly and Biff, my knowledge hasn't made me a millionaire. 'Think, McFly! Think!' Far from it, let me tell you. I've had the odd flutter over the years and rarely won. I suppose that's the beauty of football. It's just so unpredictable. Still, I would never bet serious money. It would only be a bit of fun, particularly if I was down the pub with some mates. Placing £2 on Kevin Davies to be first goal scorer just added a little bit of spice to a game I wasn't invested in. Now and again, the bet would come in and I might win a few quid. It barely covered the drinks for the afternoon, but it felt like winning the lottery. I'd celebrate a Kevin Davies goal against Palace like a last-minute United winner at Old Trafford.

My favourite bets of all were always accumulators. My

friends and I would gather around the newspaper and try and pick out winners across all the leagues. Our primary motivation was to have some fun and make a bit of money. But it also helped us learn more about the game and have us cheering on Morecambe to get an equaliser at Plymouth. Often, it's the bigger teams that let you down, though. I had one bet a few years ago where all my results had come in. I just needed Bayern Munich to beat a shitty little team I'd never heard of at home and I'd be a couple of hundred pounds richer. Of course, they lost. Bloody prats.

Anyway, even if your team isn't playing, keep an eye out for other teams or players you might like. Take some joy in them doing well. Lower your blood pressure. Let me tell you, being Old Trafford's angriest man will do you no good.

## IT'S A FUNNY OLD GAME

As Jimmy Greaves used to say, 'Football is a funny old game, Saint.'

What a legend he was. Jimmy Greaves was not only one of England's greatest footballers of all time but also one of our best pundits. Even today, I watch old shows of *Saint and Greavsie* on YouTube. As I write, I've actually just watched a show from March 1988, with highlights of Mark Hughes playing for Bayern Munich against Real Madrid.

A big part of Jimmy Greaves's appeal is that he knew the game could be a lot of fun. We forget that sometimes. We get far too caught up in the result or politics at our club. No matter how seriously you take football, we all need to remember every now and then that it can be a bloody funny and ridiculous game. Here are some of my favourite moments that always raise a smile.

Birmingham City's David Dunn thinking he is prime Ronaldinho will always be funny. In a derby game against Villa in October 2003, he tried to copy the Brazilian maestro by executing a rabona, basically kicking the ball from behind his standing leg. Instead, like a right pillock, he kicked his leg, missed the ball and staggered to the floor in front of thousands of howling Villa fans. That'll teach you, my old son. Thanks for the laughs, but stick to the basics. Then again, the year before, Villa keeper Peter Enckelman had made his own embarrassing cock-up. As the ball was thrown back to him from a throw-in, he somehow missed it and let it trickle into an empty net, making himself look about as useful as a solar-powered torch.

Then there was poor Phil Babb. As someone who missed out at Northampton Town because of a sore nutsack, I feel this more than most. In a game against Chelsea, as he slid towards goal to try and keep out Pierluigi Casiraghi's shot, he ended up slamming himself into the post, spreadeagled. It's even funnier watching it in slow motion. You get to see the exact moment he knows it's not only going to be a goal, but he's also never going to be a dad again. Fucking hell, Phil. Just let it go in. It's not worth it.

Everyone rightly had a pop at Paolo Di Canio after being sent off and then pushing referee Paul Alcock in 1998. For that, the loco Italian earned himself an 11-game ban. Looking back, though, so much of it is bloody funny. Nigel Winterburn is trying to be all hard, barking away in Di Canio's face. Yet, when the unhinged Italian makes a move towards him, Winterburn totally shits himself. Of course, the funniest moment is the push itself. Yes, Di Canio puts his hands on the referee, but it's pretty pathetic. It's not enough for any grown man to fall over. And yet Alcock hams it up to the max. He's like Del Boy falling through the bar in *Only Fools and Horses.*

Now, I don't get any pleasure in watching someone hurt themselves, but sometimes you can't help but laugh. Take Bury's Chris Brass, for instance. In a game against Darlington in 2006, he tried to clear the ball out of his own penalty area but somehow smashed it into his own face. That's funny enough, but then the ball cannoned off his nose and into the goal. Absolutely fantastic. Talk about shitting your own bed. If that wasn't bad enough, he broke his nose in the process. It's like asking Richie from *Bottom* to try and score the ultimate own goal.

This next one, though, really was a work of art. I'd hang it on my wall if I could. Harry Redknapp once said that his wife Sandra could have scored a chance that Darren Bent had missed. It seems this might have given the gods an idea to give poor Darren a helping hand. While playing for Sunderland in 2009, Bent took a swipe at a shot that looked to be trickling harmlessly into Liverpool goalkeeper Pepe Reina's hands. But at that exact moment, a beach ball found itself in the middle of the penalty area. The next thing you know the ball's only gone and hit the beach ball and deflected past the bewildered Reina and into the goal. Where are your notes on that, Rafa? What makes this even funnier is a beach ball had as many assists that season as Jack Wilshere.

In their continued service to comedy, Liverpool also gave us another moment for the Twitter meme lords to salivate over in 2014. At the time, Liverpool was heading towards the title but needed to win every game as the season came to a close. After a monumental win against rivals Man City, the cameras captured Steven Gerrard gathering the team into a huddle, roaring, 'This doesn't slip now!' Oh yes, it does, Stevie, my old son. Two games later, Gerrard slipped when trying to pass the ball as the last man, and Chelsea's Demba Ba took full advantage. Liverpool lost the game, and their title challenge was in the bin – and with it any chance of Gerrard ever winning the Premier League. It's something I can watch again and again. Hilarious. After a hard day I like to light the candles, lather myself up and stick that on. Stuff Pornhub. Give me Gerrard slipping any day.

While matters on the ball can be bloody funny, sometimes nature likes to get involved as well. Sorry to bring this up again, Gary, but during a group game against Ireland in the 1990 World Cup, Gary Lineker pooed his pants on national television. It's the type of stuff you have nightmares about. It's not even during a run-of-a-mill game that no one cares about. It's the World Cup finals, with the whole country watching. Of course, everyone was really mature, forgot all about it, and never mentioned it to Gary ever again . . .

It's a bit of a disaster, really. A girl I went to secondary school with met a similar fate during a race in the school sports day. While running in her best whites, a poo slipped out in full view of pupils, teachers and parents. I mean, there's just no coming back from that. It's the walk of shame and then some.

Most players can manage to play a game of football without pooing their pants. Yet even then, they're not safe. During a match against Swansea in 2014, Ashley Young was minding his business when a bird pooed directly into his mouth. In fairness, it was a hell of a shot. Best of all, Ashley didn't seem to mind. He just licked his lips and got on with it as if it was a delicious chicken tikka masala. At least it's protein, Ashley, or I think it is.

Now most of us like a drink or two at the football. Norwich City owner Delia Smith is no different. The big difference is that the rest of us can shout nonsense from the stands without anyone noticing. Delia, on the other hand, likes to walk into the centre circle at half-time, grab a microphone and shout at the fans, 'Let's be having you!' Have an early bath, Delia, for fuck's sake. It was like watching your mum on Christmas Day after a few too many Proseccos, trying to get a game of Pictionary going.

However, some things in football are so inexplicable that they can only be explained if a player has been at the vodka before the game. How else can you explain what happened to Zaire's Mwepu Ilunga in a 1974 World Cup game against Brazil? While Brazil lined up a free kick, Mwepu broke away from the Zaire wall and thunderbastarded the ball away. He then shrugged his shoulders with a look of pure innocence, as if he didn't know what the big deal was. To be fair, it's probably the only time he touched the ball in the whole game.

Of course, some of the funniest moments in football involve us fans. One of my favourites is Wealdstone supporter Gordon Hill getting a bit lairy towards Whitehawk FC fans in 2013. The phrases have since become legendary; 'If you want some, I'll give it to ya . . . You've got no fans.' For this, Hill earned the nickname 'The Wealdstone Raider' and has gone down in meme folklore. It still gets me every time I see it.

Then there was Karl Power, who in 2001 somehow blagged his way into the United pre-match team photograph before the game against Bayern Munich. There he is, in full kit, standing next to Andy Cole, and no one bats an eyelid. I suppose Cole thought Power might at least be better than Ronnie Wallwork. However, when Gary Neville threatened to rumble him just seconds before the photo was taken, Power told him, 'Shut it, Gary, you grass, I'm doing it for [Eric] Cantona.' We all are, Karl. We all are.

The one fan moment that gets me every time, though, is during a 2018 game between Plymouth and Bristol Rovers. When Plymouth scored, a fan in a wheelchair got to his feet and celebrated. Plymouth were so good they were making miracles happen.

Just remember, as a football fan if you don't laugh, you'll only bloody cry. So, get as much joy from the game as you can.

## MENTAL HEALTH

Football can be an emotional game. A bad result can send you spiralling into a bad mood for days. I remember a Leeds fan I used to work with told me that if they lost on the weekend, it would take him into the middle of the following week to get over it. This wasn't for a cup final or anything major. This was for every single game. Football is meant to be an escape, but sometimes it can get too much. You're not Arsenal circa 2004. You're not invincible. There's only so much crap you can watch.

It's not just the dismay and frustration of a bad result that can get to fans. Abuse on social media between fans is shocking. People say things to each other that they would never say in the street. The terraces in the seventies and eighties could be horrible places. Racist, homophobic and hurtful chants were freely hurled at opposing fans and players, often with a threat of violence. Thankfully, in this country at least, we've mostly eradicated this in stadiums. But it seems that this vile element has now transferred to social media. Rather than such abuse being limited to match day, as it was in the past, it is now a 24/7 carousel of shit. You can't escape it unless you avoid social media altogether.

Now if you watch my videos, you can probably tell that football fucks me off on a regular basis. I also get my fair share of trolling. Over the years, I've been called all sorts of names, and, to be honest, much of it is water off a duck's back. Yet, when I first got started, it did upset me. Probably the worst thing I can remember is when certain individuals 'outed' me and said that my real name was Brent Di Cesare and that I was from Nottingham. It's true, of course, but it just felt like an invasion of privacy, with people out to get me. I explained the situation straight away. I had never tried to fool anyone. I had only used the alias Mark Goldbridge because I was working for the police at the time and felt uneasy using my real name. It was all perfectly innocent, but then some people tried to use it against me. I've never got to the bottom of it all, but apparently it came from a Liverpool website, and it had been planted there by a rival YouTuber who'd always had an axe to grind. I'm more than hardened to this sort of thing now, but that did rock me at the time.

The thing is, I went into all of this quite naively and innocently. I had no ambitions for fame and money. I just like to talk about football and have some fun with fellow fans. I had no grand ambitions or concept that what I did would ever become so popular. There was no big investment or plan. I've just winged it every step of the way. I'm always going to be grateful to do what I do, and for the most part, it's been a blast, but social media loves a pile-on. I've learned that once it begins, you need to step away. You can't answer every single person posting abuse and win every argument. Some people are just desperate to see you fail and will happily stab you in the back. People say it comes with the territory, and I get that, but I must admit, it does get lonely sometimes. You've got to have a thick skin to get through it when it does kick off.

Over time, I've learned things that can help to lift my mood if I'm feeling down. Being in a routine and working hard on a project keeps me occupied in a healthy way. Getting out of the house also helps. I film most of my content from a studio at home. This can mean I rarely leave the house. I've learned that I need fresh air. I need real interaction with others. Otherwise, I don't feel right. As much as I can, I try to go for a walk, make plans with my friends or go outside for a kick-around with my children. I've also learned other 'tricks' that have helped me deal with anxiety, things like Wim Hof breathing techniques, which seem to calm me down, or even ice baths.

Thankfully, we are all getting better at talking about these issues. In the past, if a man was struggling mentally, he'd be afraid to open up about it. It just wasn't the done thing. You'd be told to 'man up', which is a phrase I hate. Now, there's a lot more awareness of mental health. We see players openly talk about it a lot more. Only recently, Burnley striker Lyle Foster announced he was taking some time away from the game to seek treatment for his mental health. I hope this encourages fans to also realise that we're all human. Life's difficult. It's not fair at times. You'd be surprised how many people feel the same as you do but don't talk about it. I get so many DMs from people who are struggling with things in their life. Football is meant to help us escape that, to make us happy and to connect with others. If it doesn't, then take a step back for a bit. Catch your breath. It'll still be there when you're good and ready. Remember, no matter who you support, the football family always has each other's backs. Never forget that. You're not alone.

# 9

# PROFESSOR GOLDBRIDGE'S FOOTBALL UNIVERSITY

Being a football fan is hard bloody work. Just think of the hundreds of thousands of hours you put into the game. Not just watching it. Reading about it. Analysing it. Talking about it. Thinking about it. Wanking . . . if things are going really well. In our lifetime, we might devote more hours to football than anything else. Some will think that's a waste of time. 'Think of all the other things you could be doing instead,' you hear your mum cry. If you had sacked off football, you could have found the time to do something really useful, like learn another language or study for a degree. Speaking as someone who failed their GCSEs, didn't take my A levels and still came out the other side, I'm here to tell you that being a football fan is the greatest education anyone could ask for.

Football has given me far more than any degree ever could. Stuff your doctorates up your arses. They're a waste of bloody time. When I think back to some of the pivotal moments in my life, they've come about because of football. Whether that's bonding with my dad, making friends or building a career. You can't learn that at the Bullingdon Club, although it does help if you want to run the country. Stop it now, Mark. You're not Gary Lineker.

Anyway, thanks to the Football University, these modules have helped me, and millions of others, navigate the murky waters of life, and might just help you to. Lessons are now in session. Please take your seats. And stop making those faces at the back. You look a right prat.

## SOCIOLOGY

It's Christmas Eve 1914. The First World War has been raging for five months. Hundreds of thousands of people have already died. After another day of fighting in the trenches on the Western Front, there seems to be no end to this madness in sight, like watching United under Van Gaal.

Then, almost like magic, the shooting stops. The sound of 'Silent Night' echoes across the darkness. Soldiers from both sides bravely stick their heads above the trenches and walk into No Man's Land, where they meet halfway. Rather than attempt to kill one another, like David Batty and Graeme Le Saux, they put down their weapons. Talking to each other and sharing food and drink, the soldiers show each other pictures of their loved ones before a football magically appears. With hostilities temporarily halted, the two enemies play a mass football match in the middle of the battlefield. Someone must be cutting onions. Bloody football, hey.

The First World War Christmas football match has gone down in history as the ultimate example of enemies putting down their weapons to come together. I'm not saying I've ever fought in the trenches and had this issue. But the point is, football is often a great leveller. Just think of all those times you've been cornered by some boring bastard – at a party, having your hair cut, in a taxi, at school or on a date even. You might be a different age, from a different background or even from a different country. Sometimes it can get real fucking weird, both of you scrambling around for some kind of common ground, like two dogs sniffing a turd in a sandpit. Just relax. Break out the football bread. 'Who do you support then?' Or 'Fucking hell, did you see the game on the week-end?' Not hard, is it? Moments before, there was awkwardness. Now, there's a glint in both of your eyes. Quickly, you're off to the races, both on safe ground, and the conversation is flowing. Before you know it, you're debating why Mark Goldbridge is the greatest thing that's ever happened to football.

You don't even have to support the same team to connect. We've all had great conversations with rival fans in the most unusual places. In 2004 I was in a bar in Mallorca, watching England play in the Euros, when I struck up a conversation with a guy next to me who happened to be German and supported Bayern Munich. We chatted for ages about United beating them in 1999 and how they won the Champions League a few years later. So, everyone's a winner, right? Except he confided that despite that win, the way Munich lost the final in 1999 still traumatised him. I enjoyed hearing this. Don't give Goldbridge the bait. He'll snap your hands off every time. I'm sure it was therapy for the Munich fan to get this out of his system as well. There, there, Günter. Just cry it out on Goldbridge's shoulders. Shall we talk about Ole Gunnar Solskjaer again? You don't have to be strong anymore. Let it all out.

I'm not just talking a load of sentimental bollocks here, either. There's been countless scientific studies that back all of this up. Being a football fan not only increases social opportunities but also helps to encourage social connectedness, belonging and affiliation. There you go. Swivel on some of that. Time and again, this has happened right throughout my life. After my parents' divorce, it was watching football with my dad that helped cement our relationship. I grew close to my grandad because of our love for Manchester United. At school, I was destined to be the class weirdo, but playing football allowed me to make friends far more easily, even if I was still a bit strange. So many of the enduring friendships in my life are thanks to football. It has given me the confidence to speak to people I might never have done otherwise, and from there, a beautiful friendship has flourished, creating many of my most treasured memories. See, I'm not just a heartless bastard.

Football is also a form of magic. You don't have to go to The Haçienda and drop a load of pills to hug a stranger and tell them you love them. Football is far more pure than that. It's an outlet for our emotions which we might not otherwise have. In the ecstasy of a last-minute goal, you jump around like a lunatic, feel that cathartic release of emotion and then experience a shared bond as you embrace a fellow fan you've never met before. They might smell of BO and wear Tesco clothes, but the point is it doesn't matter. You're connecting like two fellow human beings.

We'd never do it sober at any other time of our lives. In fact, we'd cross the street to avoid most of these people. There's something wonderful about that, though, isn't there? For a moment, football can make us all equal. It's Friends Reunited, and then some.

## POLITICS

Don't worry. I'm not about to go all Gary Lineker on you. There isn't a GoFundMe request at the end for some cause or details about any march. This is just to make the point that thanks to football, you might know more about the world than if you tuned into an episode of *Newsnight*.

Let's take the 1998 World Cup as an example. During the group stages, the world watched with bated breath as the USA faced Iran. It's a shit game on paper. Who really gives a toss? But then you find out the two countries are mortal enemies. Think Andy Cole and Teddy Sheringham, and then add Roy Keane in the middle to stir the pot. This was the first time the two countries had ever faced each other in sports. At the time, I knew very little about politics. In fact, I'd have struggled to tell you who the prime minister was, but it was only in the build-up to the game that I understood why this was such a big deal.

Those naughty Yanks had apparently supported the overthrow of Iran's elected government in 1953 after it had nationalised its oil industry. This went down as well as a fart at a funeral. Following decades of fucking each other off, 52 American diplomats were then taken hostage in Tehran in 1979. America decided to shove this up Iran's arse by supporting Iraq during its war in the 1980s. Talk about throwing oil on the fire. By 1998, tensions were still higher than at an Oasis reunion.

Before the game, both teams were expected to walk towards each other to shake hands. Except the Iranian players were forbidden by their government from doing this. With everyone shitting themselves, it was agreed that only the Americans would walk towards the Iranians to shake hands. In return, the Iranian players would hand them white roses, a symbol of peace. Lovely stuff. Now, let's get on with the football.

After all of these niceties, I grabbed my popcorn and waited for the fireworks to erupt. Go on. Kick each other, ya prats. Fight! Fight! Fight! It was bloody boring, though. Nothing really happened other than Iran causing an upset and winning 2–1. The result wasn't the point, though. And no one was going to go all Roy Keane with so much riding on it. Arguing the toss over a free kick might kick off a war. The way the game had been played was what truly mattered. As US defender Jeff Agoos said, the players did 'more in 90 minutes than the politicians did in 20 years'. To be fair, you could say the same about Torquay vs Exeter when compared to most governments. Enough now, Mark. Rein it in.

Anyway, while I had been hoping for both teams to really go at it, it was only through football that I learned any of the political background. Before the game, I barely knew anything about any conflict between Iran and America. I certainly didn't watch the news or read about world politics in any newspaper at that age. Maybe it was mentioned in school, and I wasn't paying attention. Either way, over the years, watching football has helped to educate me about political and religious issues between cities and countries throughout the world.

I've learned about drug lords in Colombia following the death of Andrés Escobar after the 1994 World Cup. Watching Rangers vs Celtic has educated me about the religious divide in Glasgow and beyond. I've also learned about human rights issues in Qatar after the World Cup was staged there in 2022. Following the Busby Babes' story and their early escapades in Europe allowed me to learn about 'The Iron Curtain' and the Cold War. If I was made to learn about these things as a part of any school lesson, I would have fucked it off. Yet, I paid attention because they were attached to something I love. Now, it might not have gotten me any GCSEs, but neither did over a decade in school.

## GEOGRAPHY

When I was young, there was a village called Tollerton near where I lived. Due to the similarity in the names, I used to think this was where Tottenham played. I was, therefore, always confused when we drove through this tiny place, and I couldn't see White Hart Lane anywhere. I would swivel my neck repeatedly, looking for this big football stadium, only to see a bunch of farmers instead. To be fair, there probably are lots of similarities. Anyway, it was only thanks to this confusion that I realised that Tottenham and Arsenal (a name I always found funny) were both based in London.

Over the years, I've learned far more about geography through football than any lesson. During the 1990 World Cup, I was confused when commentators kept referring to

England playing the Netherlands, Holland or the Dutch. Were they playing two different teams on the same night, or were there three names for the same country? When I asked my mum to provide me with the answer, she stared at me blank-faced. 'Have you cleaned your room, Mark!?' Finally, my curiosity led me to the school library. At last, I found a book that set me straight. As I had suspected, Holland and the Netherlands are two very different things. Holland is a province famous for its capital Amsterdam and, as my mum would say, stag parties on the wacky backy, while the Netherlands is the name of the entire country, famous for windmills and clogs. Something like that, anyway.

Following United in Europe, as well as England, meant I was always learning something new. I didn't have a clue where Cameroon was before England played them in 1990. I also knew nothing about Rotor Volgograd and Russia before United played them in 1995. After they knocked us out of Europe, I wish that had remained the case. Watching Italian football on Sunday afternoons also meant I'd want to know where Sampdoria or Juventus played. Sometimes, *Gazzetta Football* would even visit the regions and you'd learn about the Tuscan vineyards or the Roman Colosseum. Again, I was never going to watch a travel show, but I was more than interested to know where Del Piero played his football and in that way learn about the city. It was even better when Gazza was involved, taking viewers on chaotic trips through Rome and beyond. It says something that I learned more from Gazza about geography than from any teacher.

# FOREIGN LANGUAGES

Some of us give it a bit of Del Boy when we're abroad. Chateauneuf du Pape! We think we know the lingo and give it our best shot. Others are far more cultured. Following our club and country around Europe and beyond, we've picked up a few phrases and can get by. But the true fan is already fluent in another language altogether: football.

To the uninitiated, speaking 'football' might as well be speaking Swahili. It can make absolutely no sense. Fans can have an entire conversation, apparently talking total nonsense, but know exactly what the other is saying. Like any language, 'football' has grown over many decades, and to be able to converse, you've got to keep up with the kids. Here are some of my favourite phrases to help you get by when speaking to any fan.

## THE 12TH MAN

No, this doesn't mean a team can actually sneak an extra man onto the pitch, as much as Sheffield United might need them. It's metaphorical and can be used in two different ways. Sometimes, it's used to refer to the crowd, which inspires and bolsters their team almost as if they have an extra man on the field. Other times it's used to refer to a particularly shit referee who is acting like the opposition's 12th man. Either way, it can be a term of endearment or frustration. Referee Howard Webb was often accused of being United's 12th man. Fergie knew how to butter him up by consistently calling him 'the best referee in the country'. It bloody worked and all. In 2011 Liverpool's Ryan Babel was so incensed by this that he even posted a mocked-up photo of Webb wearing a United shirt. While Webb denies any bias, he has admitted he wrongly gave a penalty to United when 2–0 down to Spurs, only for Ronaldo to score and start a comeback that resulted in a 5–2 win. You could blame Howard Webb. But equally, it is Spurs, so . . .

## GAME OF TWO HALVES

This has three very different meanings, so try to keep up. Football is literally a game of two 45-minute halves. There are also two halves to a football pitch, divided by a halfway line. But this term usually refers to a team making a total cluster-fuck of a game. They might have been cruising in the first half, but then fuck it up in the second. More often than not, this phrase can be levelled at Spurs. I'm trying not to pick on you, Spurs. I'm really not. I've actually really enjoyed watching the Big Ange revolution this season, but your record in second-halves isn't the best, is it? Come on now. Let's be honest. Don't take it out on Goldbridge for spitting bare facts.

GOAT

This is a newer addition to the football lexicon, and you usually see it asked on social media: who is the GOAT? Congrats if you've worked out we're not talking about farmyard animals here. GOAT is an acronym, which of course means 'greatest of all time'. Most often it is applied to the rivalry between Cristiano Ronaldo and Lionel Messi. This grinds my bloody gears. It really does. Every time you post anything, there'll always be a fanboy from one of these camps polluting my feed. So, here it goes. Let Goldbridge settle this for you once and for all.

As I write, Ronaldo has scored 732 club goals and Messi has scored 715. Bloody ridiculous. In 2014–15, Ronaldo scored a career-best 61 goals, and in six consecutive seasons scored 50 goals or more. How has that even happened? It's obscene. Then, there's Messi. In 9 of his 17 seasons at the Nou Camp, the Argentine wizard scored over 40 goals, including 73 in 60 games in 2011/12. That's just taking the piss. Who was he playing? Derby County every week?

Now let's take a look at their records for their countries. Ronaldo is currently the all-time record international goal scorer with 127 goals, compared to Messi's 106. However, while Ronaldo won the Euros in 2016, Messi memorably won the grandest prize of all in 2022 with the World Cup. Whatever way you slice it, these two aren't even human.

To put this insanity into perspective, as I currently write, Erling Haaland will need to score at least 42 goals a season for the next 15 years to surpass Messi's and Ronaldo's current records. We took this nonsense for normal. It's not. We won't see their like again, but for a period of time, we were able to watch them every week inspire each other to new heights.

Who's better? My heart always says Ronaldo. What he achieved at United in his first spell was phenomenal, and he's proved himself in three big leagues. However, my head says Messi. He's the full package. He's the ultimate goal scorer and playmaker in one. Still, why choose? Just enjoy them both. Put your Cookie Dough on top of your Phish Food and tuck in.

## GROUP OF DEATH

Don't panic. Football hasn't gone all *Squid Games* just yet. FIFA isn't about to sentence teams to death if they finish bottom of their group. Although, in some cases that might not be a bad idea. It would certainly get a performance out of André Onana. In reality, it just means a tough group in a competition like the Champions League or the World Cup. During our run to the treble in 1999, United was in a group that included Barcelona and Bayern Munich. In the bloody group stages! In contrast, when City won the competition, they faced Sevilla and Copenhagen. I'm just saying, alright. Liverpool also encountered a 'Group of Death' in 2021, facing Porto, Atlético Madrid and AC Milan. Welcome to the party, pal. Fair fucks to them, though; they won all six games!

## YOUR 'MANCHESTER UNITEDS'

This phrase is usually spoken by someone with an inferiority complex who is admitting their club is dogshit in comparison to others. That's what they want you to think, anyway. They're usually just playing silly buggers, trying to lower expectations and lessen the pressure on themselves. They hope it will give them an excuse when their team inevitably loses. I know what you're doing. So, I'll clear this up now. What they really mean to say is, 'We're a tin pot club, who play like a bunch of farmers, and I'm so fucking jealous of those mighty Reds.'

## LOST THE DRESSING ROOM

Yes, you guessed it, we haven't actually lost the dressing room here. Don't panic, players aren't going to have to get changed in the car park. As much as we'd like certain managers and players to lose it, it is still there. This usually refers to a manager who can't get a performance out of his team anymore. Exhibit A: Ole Gunnar Solskjaer. After losing 5–0 at Old Trafford to Liverpool in October 2021, the team followed that up the next month with a 4–1 loss to Watford. At that point, it's time to put the old dog out of its misery. They're done. Dressing room well and truly lost.

## PARKING THE BUS

As I said, most words in any language come about because of a specific incident. Most of those origins are lost to time, but in 'football', we can still pinpoint when an exact phrase was created. We can give credit to José Mourinho for this one. When manager of Chelsea he described Tottenham's style of play against them as 'parking the bus'. Essentially, putting every player behind the ball and playing ultra-defensively. The gaslighting little fucker. Pot. Kettle. Black.

If any team's tactics can be described as 'parking the bus', it's a José Mourinho team. Most famously, he did this when managing Inter Milan against Barcelona in the Champions League in 2010. His tactics were so defensive that Mourinho admitted, 'We didn't park the bus. We parked the plane.' It might be effective in the short term, but after a few seasons of watching this, your eyes and brain are well and truly bleached.

## NOISY NEIGHBOURS

Like the example above, the origins of this phrase are still fresh in the memory. It was first used in 2009 when Sir Alex Ferguson used it to describe Manchester City. In effect, it means a rival who does nothing but make a lot of noise. They speak so much shit that if you gave them an enema, you could bury them in a matchbox. Let's see how much noise they make when they have to finally explain those 115 charges for financial misconduct.

## A PHOTO OF A CORNER FLAG

Like any established language, it's not just about words. The ancient Egyptians used hieroglyphics to communicate, and in centuries to come, any academic studying 'football' will also have a series of images to decipher. For instance, a photo of a corner flag posted on a club's social media account might appear confusing. However, if your club posts this photo, then some serious shit is about to go down. More often than not, it means the manager has been sacked. Fuck knows why clubs have gone with a corner flag for this, though. The team bench would be more appropriate, or for some a firing squad.

# MANAGEMENT

This one has always stood me in good stead. When I'm cluster-fucking the fuck out of a situation and about to lose my shit, I ask, what would Sir Alex do? He sure as fuck isn't getting sacked on his own *FIFA* game like I've been, that's for sure.

When Sir Alex Ferguson took the manager's job at Manchester United in 1986, the club was on its arse. Marooned in the bottom three, it had been 19 years since we had last won the title. By the time Sir Alex retired in 2013, he had won 13 Premier League titles and 25 other domestic and international trophies, including two Champions Leagues. Best of all, Liverpool were knocked off their perch. Without realising it, my childhood and early adulthood were spent watching a masterclass in management. So stuff your Harvard degrees; you can learn more about management just by studying the master.

Right from the start, Sir Alex weeded out the troublemakers, the shirkers and the drinkers. Even if they were great players, it didn't matter. Paul McGrath and Norman Whiteside, thanks for everything but off you pop. High standards and values were instilled throughout the club. If you failed to meet them, then you were on your bike faster than Lance Armstrong and a belly full of drugs. Everyone was expected to have a winning mentality. If anyone complained or challenged Sir Alex's authority, he responded with the full force of the notorious Fergie 'hairdryer'. If you somehow survived that and still didn't pipe down, then you were either mental or Roy Keane. Either way, you were out. Over the years, top players like Roy Keane, David Beckham, Jaap Stam and Ruud van Nistelrooy were all sold once they stepped out of line. The success of the club came before any individual.

While Sir Alex aimed to sign good players, he also liked to sign 'bad losers'. Just think of the likes of Keane, Schmeichel or Cantona. They'd murder their own mothers over a game of tiddlywinks. They also set high standards for others to follow. Not just in games but even in training sessions. Every single day, you had to be at it. Ferguson also set an example for his players to follow. First to arrive and last to leave. All of this took time, but eventually, Ferguson's strategy paid off, and he won his first title with United in 1993.

Although Sir Alex created a winning environment, he wasn't interested in quick fixes. People like Mourinho and Conte can come into a club, spend millions, win a few trophies and be gone in a few years, leaving nothing sustainable in their place. Ferguson was different. He wanted sustained success, especially if he was going to put the all-conquering Liverpool in the bin once and for all. Signing good players was all well and good, but finding and nurturing young talent has always been in Manchester United's DNA. Since 1937 there has been a home-grown player in every United squad. That's bloody incredible when you think about it. But the club had taken its eye off the ball in recent years. When Ferguson arrived, only one player in the squad was under 24 years old. The talent well was running dry and the club was having to spend a huge amount to sign players instead, such as Terry Gibson for £500,000 and Garry Birtles for £1.2 million. I mean, who's signing those bloody cheques? It would be today's equivalent of paying £80 million for Harry Maguire or £75 million for Jadon Sancho. Hold on a minute, I see a pattern emerging here . . .

Wasting little time, the scouting system was overhauled. There was a newfound emphasis on attracting the best talent in the country to the club. Ferguson often met these young players himself. This personal touch persuaded many youngsters to sign when they might have had better offers elsewhere. Sir Alex might have thought this was below him, that he might not even be in a job by the time the kids were ready for the first team, but this made him stand out from the opposition. It took incredible patience, but the likes of Giggs, Beckham, Scholes, the Neville brothers and Nicky Butt eventually flourished for United and England, winning multiple trophies and saving the club a fortune. There was also an added benefit to this.

As they had come through the ranks at United they all upheld the standards and values instilled in them. 'Don't fuck around, alright. This shit is working!' This let any new signings know what was expected in the process, bringing ever more stability and consistency. They also showed far more loyalty to Ferguson and the club, as he was the one who had given them their chance and was almost a father figure to them. Plus, they were probably bloody terrified of him.

Yet even when the team was doing well and winning trophies, Ferguson was never afraid to break it up. Just look what he did in 1995, when big-name players like Kanchelskis,

Hughes and Ince were sold. A year later, United won the double. Just a few years after the treble triumph in 1999, Ferguson again went through a painful rebuild, with Keane, Schmeichel, Stam and Beckham all departing. In 2008 United were again champions of Europe, led by new boys Rooney, Ronaldo, Ferdinand, Vidić and Tevez. He seemed to instinctively know when a team's cycle was coming to an end, and would act just before age or complacency set in. Never be satisfied and sit still. You're not Jordan Henderson. Always be moving forward.

Managing a group of young, famous athletes, often earning huge amounts of money, might prove difficult for some. Certainly, in his early years, Sir Alex was renowned for the hairdryer form of management to keep egos in check and standards high. Yet, when necessary, he also showed a softer side. In 1995, after Eric Cantona received a nine-month ban for flykicking some gobshite at Selhurst Park, he fled to Paris and contemplated retirement. Sir Alex took the time to write and speak to him, encouraging him to return rather than lambast and humiliate him. When Cantona eventually returned, he was the catalyst for the club winning another double. The same happened with David Beckham in 1998. After he had been sent off for England in the World Cup and was getting death threats, some idiots were even hanging effigies of him outside pubs. Ferguson had his own issues with Beckham's level of celebrity and focus at times. However, he immediately called Beckham and told him the club would protect him. The rest of the country might have been baying for his blood, but United would be his sanctuary. That season, Beckham came second in the Ballon d'Or and was an integral player as United won the treble. And we did it without racking up 115 charges against us. We just needed 92. The class of '92.

As I've already mentioned, time and again, Sir Alex's teams snatched victory from the jaws of defeat in so-called 'Fergie Time'. It happened so often that some rival fans saw it as a conspiracy or that United was just lucky. But United fans knew different. While Ferguson cultivated a winning environment and signed players who hated to lose, he also planned for all eventualities. In training, he would work on how his team would chase a goal in the dying minutes of games. It wasn't just a case of throwing everyone forward and hoping for the best. There was a method to it. He told his players not to panic. Just carry out what they had worked on for such a scenario. His detailed preparation and willingness to gamble meant his players were better prepared in the final moments of games than most other teams.

Some managers burn bright for a period of time, then slowly fade away. Just look at José Mourinho, who has been fighting against the dying of the light for almost a decade now. Plenty of others, as well, have had success but have been unable to sustain it over a long period. George Graham at Arsenal. Howard Kendall at Everton. Kenny Dalglish at Blackburn.

Sometimes, the game moves on and managers are unable to move with it. This is the most remarkable thing about Sir Alex's time as manager of Manchester United. Just think of all the changes in the game he faced during his 26 years at the top: the introduction of the Premier League, the three-foreign-players rule in Europe, the back pass rule, the Bosman ruling, the foreign invasion, footballers becoming more like celebrities with egos to match, billionaire foreign owners, the constant changing of styles and tactics – from long-ball British football on muddy pitches to tiki-taka on bowling greens. Despite all of these challenges, Sir Alex never stopped winning. Unlike others, he paid attention and learned to adapt, even when it was difficult and painful to do so. He was one of the first managers to introduce squad rotation, to play youngsters in cup competitions, to utilise sports science and stats and ensure that United also had the most up-to-date equipment and facilities.

It's not just Sir Alex who is an example to follow. A lot of clubs have a legendary management figure you can learn from. Clough at Forest. Shankly at Liverpool. Wenger at Arsenal. Pep at City. Watch them; learn from them. And ask yourself what they might do in a certain situation. It's amazing how channelling your inner Fergie can pay off in real life.

This concludes Professor Goldbridge's Football University. Now run free, and try not to be a prat on your way out.

# EPILOGUE

We've established that being a fan is hard bloody work. You might have even read this book and thought, *Why the hell do I bother? I'd be better off painting over a white wall with white paint on Saturday afternoons.* But every so often, all the disappointment and pain are worth it. Trust me. My moment came at precisely 21.43pm on 26 May 1999.

Yes, you guessed it. Have a prize. It's the Champions League final: United against Bayern Munich. We'd wrapped up the league and cup double a few days before with barely a scratch on us. Arsenal and Newcastle were in the bin. Now, we were going for the treble. No English club had ever won the treble before. Not even Liverpool in their pomp. It was a shot at immortality. A chance to laud it over our rivals forever. Three fingers up. Immune to all banter. Have it, Dalglish, Souness, Rush and Barry Venison. Even David Burrows can have some, as well. Your boys took a hell of a beating.

Everything that season had been building up to this: Solskjaer's last-minute winner against Liverpool, the ball going through Jamie Carragher's outstretched legs; Giggs' wonder goal against Arsenal, shirt swinging above his head; Cole and Yorke at the Nou Camp, telepathically reading each other's minds like Derren Brown; Keane dragging us to victory against Juventus, against all odds. All of this was pre-destined. There was no other way to explain it. It was as if the gods had decided that it was our time. Like *The Generation Game*, we'd already had the cuddly toy and microwave; now was the time for the Caribbean holiday. 'Nice to see you. To see you nice.' But the game was almost over, and we were fucking it up, losing 1–0 and playing crap. The way it was going, the only cup we were getting that night was a cup of tea.

I hadn't made the trip to the Nou Camp, where the game was being played, standing by the side of fellow United stalwarts, belting out, 'Giggs will tear you apart, again.' I was a skinny 19-year-old Liam Gallagher wannabe, squeezed next to other United fans on a sofa at a house party in Dublin. My girlfriend at the time had persuaded me to go. 'It'll be good craic,' she'd said. Just like she'd persuaded me to move from Nottingham to Dublin after meeting in Mallorca a year earlier. She'd been right on that one. But watching a game of this magnitude, with a bunch of strangers chatting away, not paying attention, was a disaster. I refer you to Chapter Four for how to avoid this.

As Ryan Giggs went down another blind alley, I stood and gesticulated at the TV in desperation. 'For fuck's sake,' I shouted, spilling the can of Amstel in my hand. 'What's he doing?' I turned to look at the other United fans on the sofa next to me for support. Zombie-like faces stared back. They'd given up. There were just three minutes to go, and we hadn't looked like we were going to score all night. Cole and Jesper Blomqvist were off; Sheringham and Solskjaer on. A desperate last throw of the dice but still nothing was going for us. What an absolute shitshow this had been.

A sick feeling built in my stomach. I looked around the packed room and saw someone look in my direction and mouth to his mate, 'Choking'. They were both Liverpool fans. Smirks plastered all over their bloody faces, lapping up my screams of frustration like Alan Hansen sweeping up at the back. I cursed myself. It was a stupid, stupid mistake being here. For a game like this, I should have stayed in and watched it by myself.

'Don't worry. There's always next year,' my girlfriend said, putting her hand on my shoulder, not fully understanding the gravity of the situation. I couldn't even look at her. I couldn't even make eye contact. No. There. Fucking. Won't. No English team had ever won the treble. No club had even come close. And we had a team full of kids from the academy. The class of '92. For something like this, there was no next year. This was once-in-a-lifetime stuff. But why had I been so bloody certain we would do it? Then, I realised the error of my ways.

It was the Germans. The bloody Germans. If United knew how to find a way to win, then you can bet the Germans invented the way. I should have known better. Naive. Cocky. Forgot all about Italia 90 and Euro 96 because it was a club competition. Stupid Mark. Stupid. Stupid. Stupid.

'Where are we going after this?' I heard someone ask. I couldn't believe it. It wasn't something I had contemplated. I hadn't thought about losing and what would come next. Oblivion, as far as I was concerned. Just throw me out with the bins; let the rats have me. Goldbridge is done and dusted. But then, just as I was all out of hope, Beckham won a corner. I watched on as Fergie waved for Schmeichel to get into the box. This was it. Last-chance saloon. I involuntarily stood, leaning towards the television, blocking out all noise in the party apart from Clive Tyldesley . . .

'Can they score? They always score . . .'

Beckham placed the ball down, looked up, raised his left arm, ran towards the ball and clipped it into the box. Schmeichel jumped for it . . .

'GO ON, YOU BASTARDS!' I shouted.

The ball pinballed around the box, only to be half-cleared to Giggs. He took a desperate swipe towards goal, but I saw it was going wide until . . .

'SHERINGHAM!!!!'

It's in! It's bloody in! I screamed, jumped over a coffee table, didn't know what the fuck I was doing, but somehow twisted my bloody ankle. My fucking God, it hurt, but it didn't matter. At that moment, I didn't even feel the pain. I was too busy hugging strangers, telling the Liverpool fans to swivel on it.

'FUCK OFF AND TAKE JAN MØLBY WITH YOU!'

We were alive again. Back from the dead. My ankle was now bloody hurting, but I could deal with that later. I was too busy thinking about extra time. What could Fergie do now? Did we have enough gas in the tank? We had one more sub left. Who could he bring on? Before I could complete my thoughts United had somehow won another corner. I looked at the clock in the corner of the screen. Time was almost up. We had just enough time to take it if we were quick. I barely had time to stand when Beckham again struck the ball into the box. For a moment, everything went in slow motion. Sheringham ran to the near post, flicked the ball on, then Solskjaer stretched out a leg . . .

'AND SOLSKJAER HAS WON IT!'

Euphoria. Carnage. Smash the windows in and tell the world we've done it. We've won the fucking Treble! If I could've bottled that feeling and sold it I'd have solved the world's drug problems overnight. Nothing will ever emulate that high. It was perfection. Footballing perfection. And nothing will ever come close.

Hours later, I remember being sat on a beach, the sun coming up on the horizon. I had a cigar in one hand and a bottle of whisky in another. There was a warm feeling in my stomach that life would never get any better than this. It felt like I'd completed football. All the dedication and frustration had been worth it. Picking a team, standing with them throughout the ups and downs, almost pissing myself in the hope it would conjure up a goal. Being one of thousands of fans, all sacrificing our time, money and sanity to support them. I knew it might never be as good as this again. But that was alright. It had all been worth it. We'd only bloody won the lot.

Alexa, play the Champions League music.

# REFERENCES

P. 83 – 'Boom Boom Boom' by The Outhere Brothers

P. 90 – 'Every 1's a Winner' by Hot Chocolate

P. 97 – 'Don't Look Back in Anger' by Oasis

P. 223 – *Blade Runner* (1982)

P. 242 – 'Sweet Caroline' by Neil Diamond